Receptive Music Therapy

Second Edition

by the same author

Adolescents, Music and Music Therapy
Methods and Techniques for Clinicians, Educators and Students
Katrina McFerran
ISBN 978 1 84905 019 7
eISBN 978 0 85700 376 8

of related interest

Guided Imagery & Music (GIM)
and Music Imagery Methods for Individual and Group Therapy
Edited by Denise Grocke and Torben Moe
ISBN 978 1 84905 483 6
eISBN 978 0 85700 877 0

A Comprehensive Guide to Music Therapy, 2nd Edition
Theory, Clinical Practice, Research and Training
Edited by Stine Lindahl Jacobsen, Inge Nygaard Pedersen and Lars Ole Bonde
Foreword by Helen Odell-Miller
ISBN 978 1 78592 427 9
eISBN 978 1 78450 793 0

Advanced Methods of Music Therapy Practice
Analytical Music Therapy, The Bonny Method of Guided Imagery and Music, Nordoff-Robbins Music Therapy, and Vocal Psychotherapy
Nicki S. Cohen
ISBN 978 1 84905 776 9
eISBN 978 1 78450 008 5

Collaborations Within and Between Dramatherapy and Music Therapy
Experiences, Challenges and Opportunities in Clinical and Training Contexts
Edited by Amelia Oldfield and Mandy Carr
Foreword by Rebecca Applin Warner
ISBN 978 1 78592 135 3
eISBN 978 1 78450 402 1

Receptive
MUSIC THERAPY
Techniques, Clinical Applications and New Perspectives
Second Edition

Katrina Skewes McFerran
AND
Denise Grocke

Jessica Kingsley Publishers
London and Philadelphia

First published in Great Britain in 2022 by Jessica Kingsley Publishers
An imprint of Hodder & Stoughton Ltd
An Hachette Company

1

Parts of this book were originally published in *Receptive Methods in Music Therapy* (2007) by Denise Grocke and Tony Wigram

List on page 21 is reproduced from Thompson 2011 with kind permission from Stephanie Thompson.
List on page 35 is reproduced from Wärja and Bonde 2014 with kind permission from Music & Medicine.

Front cover image source: Shutterstock®. The cover image is for illustrative purposes only, and any person featuring is a model.

A CIP catalogue record for this title is available from the British Library and the Library of Congress

ISBN 978 1 78775 610 6
eISBN 978 1 78775 611 3

Printed and bound in Great Britain by CPI Group

Jessica Kingsley Publishers' policy is to use papers that are natural, renewable and recyclable products and made from wood grown in sustainable forests. The logging and manufacturing processes are expected to conform to the environmental regulations of the country of origin.

Jessica Kingsley Publishers
Carmelite House
50 Victoria Embankment
London EC4Y 0DZ

www.jkp.com

This book is dedicated to Tony Wigram, co-author of the first edition of this book: *Receptive Methods in Music Therapy* (2007), who was an inspiring teacher, researcher, mentor and friend to so many people around the world.

Contents

Introduction

We began writing this book in the early months of 2020, at a time when the COVID-19 virus dominated the news of the world. The phrases 'social distancing' and 'isolation' became the norm, not for a small section of the community, but globally, for citizens across all cultures. As we retreated inside our homes, the process of coping became apparent. Humour was the mainstay of coping in the early weeks, rapidly spread across countries via the internet. Then there was the process of giving in to the unprecedented rules restricting our freedom.

One of the significant coping mechanisms that emerged during this time was the use of music. In Italy, opera singers sang famous arias from their home balconies to the applause of neighbours isolated inside their homes. Some joined in the singing, but mostly people listened intently, as if their feelings of isolation were lessened through the listening. Group singing in suburban streets was activated to enhance a community spirit and keep hope and motivation alive. Choirs adapted to the situation by recording songs via electronic platforms to enable people to listen to choral music. Singers achieved phenomenal success in raising money by writing songs, creating videos and holding virtual concerts.

Throughout history music has had a significant role during trying times like these. The diversity of opportunities for engaging with music includes singing, playing, composing, improvising, moving and listening intently. This book focuses on the last – how listening to music, including listening to songs and instrumental music, can bring comfort. The chapters will canvas the use of receptive music therapy across the age span and inclusive of diverse music genres. The importance of music preferences and associations with music aligns with new collaborative approaches where client and therapist together create playlists and discuss the effect of music on mood, or the meaningfulness of songs and their lyrics to the person's life situation.

WHAT HAS CHANGED SINCE 2007?

The first edition of this book was published in 2007 (Grocke and Wigram 2007). It was one of the first books to focus on experiences of music that are *receptive* rather than *active*. The argument was made then that receptive music therapy approaches are not passive – the recipient is not disengaged. Instead, the person is focused on listening as the core experience.

Much has changed in the music world since 2007. Back then, clients often relied on the therapist to bring the music to the music therapy sessions – the evolution of personal listening devices was just beginning. Now our participants have numerous devices for accessing music and they are already skilled in appropriating their preferred music. Several platforms for downloading music are available, and finding a particular song or selection of instrumental music can be almost immediate. Many participants in music therapy are already skilled in composing their own playlists, enabling the power balance in sessions to shift from expert-led to more collaborative relationships.

The neuroscience of music has also developed exponentially since 2007. Studies exploring the discrete processing of music in the brain have found their way into the popular press, and our knowledge of the effect of music on mood has generated a deeper understanding of positive changes, as well as a new understanding of the negative effects of ruminating on unhealthy music choices.

HOW IS RECEPTIVE MUSIC THERAPY PRACTISED THROUGHOUT THE WORLD?

In 2016 the Commission on Clinical Practice of the World Federation of Music Therapy (WFMT) conducted a survey of music therapists worldwide (reported in Kern and Tague 2017). There were 2495 responses, with

24.4 per cent from the USA. The survey sought information on many aspects of the practice of music therapy and included one question on music therapy techniques. Singing and vocalization, instrument playing and improvisation accounted for the most often used techniques, but listening to pre-recorded music was identified by 43 per cent of respondents, and listening to live music by 42 per cent. Many music therapists use receptive methods.

WHAT IS RECEPTIVE MUSIC THERAPY?

In the first edition published in 2007 (Grocke and Wigram 2007) we clarified that receptive music therapy is not passive. Listening to music engages people when there is an intention and purpose established by the music therapist, and music listening becomes an active ingredient in achieving that purpose. An influential music therapy theorist, Kenneth Bruscia (2014), defined 'receptive methods' as follows:

> In receptive experiences, the client listens to music and responds to the experience silently, verbally, or in another modality. The music used may be live or recorded improvisations, performances, or compositions by the client or therapist or commercial recordings of music literature in various styles... The listening experience may be focused on physical, emotional, intellectual, aesthetic, or spiritual aspects of the music, and the client's responses are designed according to the therapeutic purpose of the experience. (Bruscia 2014, p.368)

Bruscia goes on to list the purposes or goals of receptive music therapy, including the promotion of receptivity, evoking affective states, imagery and fantasies, exploring ideas and thoughts, facilitating memories and regression, relaxation, or stimulating peak and spiritual experiences (2014, p.369).

Many alternative terms are used to indicate receptive music therapy, including 'music listening', 'music-assisted relaxation' (MAR), 'music for relaxation' and 'music listening interventions' (MLI), to name a few. Remarkably, some music therapists do not consider choosing pre-recorded music as a music therapy method at all. This distinction is often made by those working in medical domains, who attribute the use of pre-recorded music to medical personnel rather than music therapists. In this discourse, the use of recorded music has been deemed 'passive', suggesting that there is no engagement with the person, often because the medical personnel would activate the music and then walk away from their patient. Dileo (1989) was at the forefront of this debate, and clarified that the main difference between music medicine and music therapy in medicine was that music therapists formed a relationship with the patient, whereas in medical settings the music was often perceived as a background to, or distraction from, medical procedures (Dileo 1989, p.23).

Distinctions need to be drawn between different approaches in receptive music therapy, and how receptive music therapy is practised alongside allied methods in active music therapy, music and imagery (MI), Guided Imagery and Music (GIM), and the Bonny Method of GIM. Table I.1 sets out aspects of these four methods.

Music therapists have undertaken an accredited tertiary training course and there are clear boundaries of practice in active and receptive music therapy when practised by qualified music therapists. However, other professionals (community musicians, music teachers, other allied health professionals, for example) may use the same methods, which blurs professional boundaries. There are clear boundaries for the Bonny Method of GIM, and accredited Bonny Method practitioners may include therapists outside music therapy, including allied health professionals, social workers, psychologists and psychotherapists.

DISTINCTIONS BETWEEN ACTIVE MUSIC THERAPY, RECEPTIVE MUSIC THERAPY, MI, GIM AND THE BONNY METHOD OF GIM

One distinction between these approaches relates to the purpose of the method. Active music therapy is expressive and outward-focused, whereas receptive methods, MI, GIM and the Bonny Method of GIM are inward-looking – the benefit is gained from embodied experiences of deeper relaxation, or insight into life problems.

Another distinction relates to the role and skills of the therapist (see

Table I.1). In active music therapy the therapist is engaged in creating the music through song singing, song writing, composing and improvisation. In receptive methods the role of the therapist is to facilitate choices of music to support each participant's therapeutic experience. The choices made by the music therapist require knowledge of pre-composed music, and an understanding of the elements of music that underpin music composition. Sometimes music therapists may improvise the music that supports receptive experiences, and so even receptive methods require an understanding of how to create music to match client need.

Skills in receptive music therapy are often taught in basic music therapy training; however, there are differences in orientations in training courses across the world, and some programmes do not include music listening in their teaching. In addition, there are an increasing number of specific MI approaches. Lisa Summer (2015) has outlined a Continuum Model that has different levels of MI experiences: supportive, re-educative and re-constructive. Fran Goldberg and Louise Dimiceli-Mitran have developed a Focused Music Imagery (FMI) approach (Dimiceli-Mitran 2020) and Margareta Wärja (2015) has developed korta musikresor (KMR; short music journeys). Each of these methods requires some degree of training beyond basic music therapy training, leading to recognized qualifications that demonstrate specific skills in using music and imagery.

Probably the most vexed aspect across the array of methods is whether the professional boundaries are clear. While qualified music therapists practise active music therapy, community musicians, music teachers and other allied health practitioners also lead singing sessions, do song writing, and compose and improvise with their group members. Various allied health professionals also use some methods that we describe as receptive music therapy, for example relaxation with music or music and imagery. There are also blurred boundaries around MI methods since the training programmes that have been developed are open to professionals outside of music therapy. For example, there are clear boundaries for the Bonny Method of GIM, which requires accreditation in order to be recognized, but not all Bonny Method therapists are music therapists. The field is diverse, but in this book, we focus specifically on how qualified and professional music therapists use music listening as part of their approach to practice.

Table I.1 Distinctions between active music therapy, receptive music therapy, MI/GIM and the Bonny Method of GIM

	Active music therapy	Receptive music therapy	Named MI/GIM approaches	Bonny Method of GIM
Purpose	Uses music for expression (singing, playing, moving) Outward-focused	Intentional/deep listening to music with or without imagery, using live or recorded music Inward-focused	Deep listening with intentional imagery focus Inward-focused	Inner exploration to deepen meaning Inward-focused
Methods/ techniques	Song singing, song writing, improvisation, music and movement	Relaxation with music Music and imagery Song sharing (listening and reflecting with discussion) Music and art, e.g., music and drawing, music collage	Continuum Model (Summer) Personal MI (Scott-Moncrieff) Focused MI (Dimiceli-Mitran and Goldberg) Korta musikresor (KMR) (Wärja) Directed Music and Imagery (DMI) Music, Drawing and Narrative (MDN) (Booth)	MI journeys that deepen inner experience; requires appropriate selections of music (often classical) as catalyst for metaphoric and symbolic imagery
Role of therapist	Actively involved in playing and singing	Facilitates the listening experience with a focus on intentional listening. Also a recipient of the listening experience. May choose the music or engage the client collaboratively for music selection	Collaboratively create playlists with the client (Continuum Model: Summer) Facilitates directive MI (Dimiceli-Mitran) Facilitates music listening with art work (Wärja)	Facilitates deep listening, helping client to engage metaphoric and symbolic imagery through dialogue Reflective role in understanding client's experience

Skill set	Competent musicians in singing, accompanying, composing and playing, with wide and diverse song repertoire Adept at facilitating improvisation (listening, matching, mirroring, extending)	Provides relaxation inductions with appropriate timing and voice tone Facilitates intentional and focused music listening that may also integrate visualizations/imagery/drawing Has knowledge of music repertoire and chooses appropriate music, or engages client collaboratively to make the choice	Has knowledge of music suitable for MI and chooses appropriate music, or engages client collaboratively to find music that matches desired imagery	Facilitates discussion to elicit focus Provides relaxation induction that leads to an altered state of consciousness Chooses GIM music programmes, often 30–40 minutes in length Facilitates dialogue with participant to deepen experience Facilitates discussion of art work, e.g., mandala drawings
Training	Basic music therapy training	Training depends on the orientation of the music therapy training course. Not all courses include receptive music therapy in the curriculum. Alternative titles might be 'Music listening', 'music-assisted relaxation' and others	Additional training in Summer's Continuum Model and Wärja's KMR	Bonny Method training over two to three years post-music therapy training
Therapist qualifications	Accredited music therapist	Accredited music therapist	No specific qualification, but training is required	Accreditation in the Bonny Method of GIM

OVERVIEW OF THE BOOK

In Chapter 1 we describe processes for deciding when it might be appropriate to choose receptive methods over active methods. We also include an imperative section on the listening skills of the therapist, and verbal communication skills needed to engage clients in describing their experiences.

Selecting music for receptive methods is presented in Chapter 2. An essential knowledge of the elements of music is required to guide therapist-led decisions across diverse music genres. We highlight genres of ambient/environmental and film music, classical art music, world music and contemporary youth music. Decisions for music choices are also guided by the readiness of the recipient, and the music therapist considers the complexity of the music and how well it is aligned with the client's experience of music and their ability to regulate emotionally.

We use a framework to present different receptive methods from Chapters 3–8, including:

- relevant concepts underpinning the method
- a description of the method
- clinical vignettes
- contraindications.

Chapter 3 introduces different levels of music listening, including intentional and focused listening through to unhealthy music listening. Suvi Saarikallio, Katrina McFerran and Christian Gold's (2015) Healthy–Unhealthy Music Scale (HUMS) is explained through vignettes. Contraindications are outlined for clients who might find listening confusing.

Playlist construction is the focus for Chapter 4, outlining how a music profile is considered in the creation of playlists for specific moods and challenges in clients' lives. Vignettes include adolescent mental health and life review.

In Chapter 5 we address the popular use of song discussion and lyric analysis, identifying different levels of analysis and ways of engaging group discussion of important topics such as social reform, relationship-building, and sensitive topics of misusing alcohol and substances.

Different types of music relaxation are explained in Chapter 6, with induction scripts provided in Appendix A. We discuss essential skills for delivering relaxation inductions to maximum effect.

Music and imagery is the focus of Chapter 7, beginning with an introduction to what constitutes imagery and the importance of the imagination in everyday life. We illustrate the use of scripts for specific purposes and applications in different age groups. We outline the interaction of music and other art media, such as in Music, Drawing and Narrative (MDN) (Booth 2005–06), and other forms of drawing with music.

There are three appendices in the book. Appendix A provides scripts of commonly used relaxation inductions suitable for clients across the age span. Appendix B lists music choices commonly used in music therapy for different age groups and specific purposes. Appendix C provides imagery scripts for children.

A note about terminology

We refer to the recipients of receptive music therapy in different ways throughout the book. Sometimes we use 'client/s', coming from Carl Rogers (1951), who introduced the term in rejection of the medicalized language of 'patients' within his person-centred approach to therapy. However, when discussing medical contexts, 'patients' is the more appropriate term. At other times, it is more appropriate to refer to people as 'participants' or 'recipients'. We will carefully distinguish these terms as appropriate for different contexts in the vignettes – consumers, patients, students and so on.

Competencies

By the time you finish this book you will have developed the following:

- understanding the different models and methods of receptive music therapy
- knowing the elements of music sufficiently well to make good choices of pre-recorded music for diverse applications of receptive music therapy

- facilitating playlist construction with clients of different ages
- recognizing healthy and unhealthy uses of music listening in clients
- recognizing clients who have difficulty in regulating emotions, and adapting receptive music therapy sessions accordingly
- providing effective relaxation inductions for children, young people and adults
- understanding imagery and the role of the imagination in everyday life
- the ability to use relaxation and imagery scripts effectively
- facilitating music and art media sessions.

Chapter 1

Foundational Skills in Receptive Music Therapy

In this chapter we introduce the idea of a Decision Tree to tailor music therapy interventions and experiences to suit the needs of participants. We also introduce the listening skills required by music therapists when working with receptive methods. We emphasize that listening is an active process: it requires attention and concentration initially, followed by an empathic response based on what the client has said or experienced. How we engage people verbally is also included in this chapter as a way of deepening the participant's experience.

MAKING DECISIONS TO USE RECEPTIVE MUSIC THERAPY

VIGNETTE: Deciding between active and receptive music therapy

Meg has been an inpatient in a cancer care ward for a few days. She is a young mother, and her prognosis is not yet known. The music therapist has been working with Meg to write a song about her family and how much she misses her two young children. The music therapist notices that Meg looks tired – she has dark circles under her eyes, and her eyes seem dull. She asks Meg how she is feeling and gets a quiet response, 'Not so good'. Then she asks if Meg would like to do some more work on the song but Meg replies, 'Not really'. She asks whether Meg would like her just to sing the song, and again, Meg shakes her head. The music therapist senses that active music therapy is not appropriate for Meg today and shifts her thinking to receptive methods. She suggests to Meg that she just play some music for a while. Meg nods. She notices that Meg's breathing pattern is slow and laboured and she tunes in to the rhythmic pattern of Meg's breathing. She plays an arpeggiated open chord on the guitar, matching the pattern of Meg's breathing. Then she vocalizes gently over the guitar accompaniment, again matching Meg's breathing. She can see Meg relaxing into the bed, taking deeper breaths, and sighing out her breath. She decides to check in with Meg and asks her how she feels now. Meg says she feels better but wants to rest – eventually Meg falls asleep.

Relaxing to music can be the sole intention of a music therapy session, or it can be used at the very end of an active music-making session. As seen in this vignette, receptive approaches might be used when the person:

- is physically or emotionally tired (or both)
- feels nauseous or confused
- is not able to concentrate on active music-making such as singing or improvising
- is in pain.

Similarly, when working with groups, receptive approaches may be used when:

- the mood of the group is flat
- the group members show little enthusiasm for active methods
- the group members are physically tired or stressed.

In Stephanie Thompson's (2011) study of group music therapy for women undergoing treatment for breast cancer, she developed a Decision Tree to guide her choice of intervention on the day. She cites Stephen Pauker and John Wong's (2005) explanation that 'the Decision Tree weighs the "risks and benefits" of alternative choices and can be modified easily to suit the changing situation' (Pauker and Wong 2005, cited in Thompson 2011, p.51). Decisions were made in Thompson's study by attending to the language used in the group, the body language of the participants and the conversation themes. Thompson (2011) then identified six criteria that led her to decide which intervention to use for the group on the day:

1. Is the mood within the group positive and energized? (*active intervention*)
2. Is the mood within the group positive, but with low energy? (*receptive intervention*)
3. Is the mood within the group ambivalent, with low energy? (*receptive intervention*)
4. Is the mood within the group reflective, but there is evidence of energy? (*either an active or receptive intervention*)
5. Is the mood within the group negative, but energized? (*active intervention*)
6. Is the mood within the group sad or disappointed, and is there low energy? (*receptive intervention*) (Thompson 2011, p.64)

Based on these criteria Thompson made decisions about which intervention to use, either to start the session (with a view to including another intervention if need be), or to use it as the sole method for the session. The choice was made from a variety of interventions, such as song writing, improvisation and song singing (active music therapy) or MI, relaxation with music and song lyric analysis (receptive methods).

LISTENING SKILLS AND ENGAGING CLIENTS VERBALLY

VIGNETTE: Using effective listening skills to engage a client verbally

A music therapist working in an aged care context uses song singing to engage her groups in active music-making. She takes requests from group members and accompanies them on guitar. One of the men in the group, Bill, has requested the song 'I did it my way', and the group has finished singing. The music therapist asks Bill what he remembers about the song (this is an open question designed to allow a range of possible answers that might stimulate discussion). Bill says he likes hearing Frank Sinatra's voice – 'He was the best singer; his voice was so smooth'. Bill then asks the music therapist whether they can hear the original version of the song so they can hear Sinatra's voice.

The therapist thinks this will enhance the group cohesion; she finds the song on a streaming platform and plays it through her portable speaker. She also knows that clients sometimes want to hear the song in the authentic voice of the original performer rather than reproduced by the group. The group listens in silence and the therapist observes each person's response: some are mouthing the words as Sinatra sings; others are gazing off into the distance. Everyone is listening intently, but the therapist notices Valerie becoming tearful. At the end of the song she approaches her and asks a focused question: 'How was that for you, Valerie, listening to Sinatra's voice? You look a little bit teary.' Valerie comments that it was her husband's favourite song, and that she misses him. The music therapist is aware that others in the group are talking about other songs that Sinatra sang. She doesn't want to diminish Valerie's comment with a dismissive statement such as 'Maybe the next song will cheer you up.' Nor can she engage in an intimate discussion with Valerie at this point, because she needs to maintain the group momentum. She says, 'I would like to hear more about that, Valerie. Perhaps we can chat after the group. I'd like to know more about your husband.' This leaves Valerie with a sense that she has been heard, and that her feelings have been validated. After the session has finished the therapist approaches Valerie and pulls up a chair to sit close to her. She gives Valerie her full attention, facing her and maintaining soft eye contact. She opens the conversation by paraphrasing what had happened: 'You were reflecting on how your husband liked that song, Valerie,' and then follows with a more focused question: 'Tell me more about him and the songs he liked to hear.'

In instances like these, the music therapist draws on verbal skills to ensure that clients can reflect on what they have heard. These skills are common to all therapists and include the ability to do the following:

- Listen attentively, by listening to what is being said rather than thinking what you might say next.
- Be comfortable in silence when participants are searching for words that they want to describe their experience.
- Facilitate dialogue through open questions, and then focused questions to help participants explore feelings and emotions.

- Reflect key words that participants say about the music, or their memories or other associations.
- Maintain an attentive and open posture, sitting across from the person, not turned away, and maintaining eye contact.

Active listening

As the term suggests, 'active' listening requires active attention by the therapist – to listen and attend to what is being said, and to be wholly present to the person while they are speaking. In normal conversation the discussion moves equally between two people, but in the therapeutic context the relationship is not equal. The client is encouraged to express their thoughts and feelings, and the role of the therapist is to support the person doing that. The therapist does not engage in the same type of self-reflection of their own life with a client, and so the relationship is not equal.

One of the fundamental requirements of 'active' listening is to attend to what is being said. This may sound both simplistic and obvious, but one of the biggest mistakes new therapists make is that they sometimes only half listen to what is being said, and then mentally turn off, or they start to compose a reply in their mind. Often the client only needs a non-committal 'uh-huh' to help them continue with what they need to say. The skill in 'active' listening is to stay focused on what the client is saying and to respond in a sensitive manner, rather than filtering only part of it. It is important to remember that active listening requires effort from the therapist to stay focused on the client and not be drawn into distracting thoughts or actions. Gerard Egan summarizes this well: 'Think: what can I hear, NOT, what can I say' (Egan 1998, p.87).

Being comfortable with silence

In active music therapy, the therapist maintains the momentum of the session by actively making suggestions and engaging in dialogue. But in receptive music therapy the client may be silent for periods of time, particularly if they are in a reflective mood – they may take a few seconds to respond to a question, for example. Therapists who are not comfortable with silence may try to fill the gaps with their own words or may show signs of their own anxiety if there is silence in therapy sessions. Being comfortable with silence, however, is essential to the development of a strong therapeutic relationship. An intuitive therapist will 'feel' the depth of connection with a client while sitting in silence, and this is part of an effective therapeutic relationship.

Clients who are depressed or grieving often cannot express how they feel in words and can be almost non-responsive or non-verbal. Other clients may be very emotional after a music experience and may not be able to put the experience into words. The therapist might offer a reflection about the silence with a comment such as 'It seems that it is difficult to talk about how you are feeling at the moment.' The therapist then has a choice of offering another music listening experience.

Attentive posture

In the vignette the music therapist approaches Valerie after the session to talk with her. She pulls up a chair and sits across from her. This enables the therapist to give Valerie her full attention. She doesn't sit in the chair next to Valerie because Valerie may not experience her as being attentive – Valerie may gaze around the room and watch what's going on rather than be engaged with the music therapist.

Eye contact

The music therapist also maintains a 'soft gaze' eye contact with Valerie. When talking with clients (between music-making or listening to music), eye contact is essential. We engage in eye contact to show interest, and to remain focused on what is being said. Sustained or intense eye contact may be uncomfortable for some people, however, and so the therapist intuitively monitors the degree of direct eye contact with the client. Essentially, the client has less eye contact with the therapist than the therapist with the client. Sometimes the client may look away. The therapist needs to sustain 'soft' eye contact so that when the client does look back to the therapist, the client sees that the therapist is still focused on them.

In summary, Table 1.1 sets out effective listening habits to enhance therapeutic engagement, compared to non-effective habits.

Table 1.1 A comparison of effective listening skills and poor listening habits

Effective listening skills	Poor listening habits
Maintaining appropriate eye contact while the client is speaking	Looking or turning away from the client, or looking 'past' them, or rapid shift in eye movement
Staying relaxed while listening to the client	Fidgeting, changing body posture or looking around the room, which indicates that the therapist is not attending fully
Being present to the client's experience	Mentally 'turning off' from what the client is saying, or thinking about a response rather than listening to what is being said
Being comfortable with silence, particularly to allow the client to find the words to express themself	Filling in the silences with their own words
Giving the client time to speak and allowing them to complete what they are saying	Interrupting the flow of language or trying to guess what the client is saying
Helping the client to understand their behaviours and feelings	Judging what the client is saying or doing, making inappropriate comments such as 'What you need to do is...', or worse, contradicting the client: 'But you said yesterday that you liked this music'
Staying focused on what the client is expressing and understanding how important it is for that person	Talking about other people's experiences, thereby diminishing the client's experience, e.g., 'Oh, everyone feels like that sometimes'
Being empathetic to the client's situation	Diminishing the importance of the client's situation by dismissing it: 'You'll feel better tomorrow' or 'Many people have the same problem'

ENGAGING CLIENTS VERBALLY

It is difficult to provide a comprehensive guide to what words to use when engaging in conversation with clients – there are far too many variables to be able to give accurate advice. Paul Nolan (2005) has outlined times when verbal interactions are needed in music therapy, including during the introductory and closing components of sessions, when finding a focus and gathering more information, for giving feedback and interpretations, as well as when helping people to understand their responses to the music.

Elizabeth Schwartz (2019) is another author who has written about 'basic verbal skills for music therapists', and considered that there are four categories of verbalizations in music therapy, including framing, exchanges, interactions and interventions (2019, p.48).

The use of verbal framing and verbal exchanges is included within most music therapy sessions. Verbalization within these categories can be helpful to orient the client towards the music and music therapy and inform them about the experiences that can be expected, for example, 'Let's listen to this selection of music and while we are listening you might like to close your eyes and let the music wash over you.' This phrase doesn't require the client to respond; it simply informs them about what is going to happen and gives some open-ended instruction about how to engage with the music.

Verbal interactions and verbal interventions, on the other hand, involve dialogue that requires the client to have the capability to use spoken language, and to be willing and able to reflect more deeply. In addition, the therapist needs to be comfortable inviting the client into deeper reflection, and sometimes the therapist needs to be comfortable hearing reflections of grief and despair, or anger and rage.

Cautions

Music therapists who are early in their career may not feel experienced enough to go more deeply into clients' experiences, and supervision may be required to develop more advanced skills. Also, some music therapists do not feel it appropriate to delve more deeply, because intuitively they feel it is not the right time, or they feel the client may not benefit from opening up more. Furthermore, it may be inappropriate to delve more deeply if the client is living with mental health issues. Our most important ethical guideline is: do no harm. When in doubt, it is best to keep the client emotionally safe. The verbal skills outlined here are core skills, on which you can build.

Verbal skills

There are different ways of engaging verbally with clients through interactions and verbal interventions: using open questions; using reflections of key words; paraphrasing what has just happened to help contain the experience for the client; using focused questions and probes to seek more information; and closure – using a summative statement to round off what has been covered.

Open questions

We use verbal processing techniques following a musical experience to gain information about what the client has experienced. 'Open' questions are preferable to 'closed' questions. A typical open question following a music experience is 'What was that like for you?', which leaves the response wide open. A more targeted question would be 'How did you feel about that?', which focuses more on the person's feelings. A closed question would be 'Did you enjoy that?' The question is closed because it invites a 'yes/no' reply. It could also be biased in a sense – it suggests that the therapist wants the client to only think of whether it was enjoyable. People may unconsciously answer 'yes' because it is implied in the question, and may feel that the therapist wants them to say 'yes'.

REFLECTING

Reflecting a client's key word or phrase is an effective way to affirm an important statement or feeling. If a client comments that the music has made them feel sad, it can be effective to reflect the word – 'Oh, sad' – using a similar tone to what the client has used. The most logical follow-up question then is 'In what way has it made you feel sad?' Reflecting the person's words or feeling state allows the client to stay in the moment and explore it more fully. In many respects this is a unique aspect of therapy – providing people with the time they need to uncover feelings at a pace that is comfortable for them.

Reflecting techniques should not be over-used, however. If the therapist simply reflects each word or statement the client makes, the client may feel the therapist is mimicking them or making fun of what is being said. But when used at the right time to highlight something important that has been said, reflections can be very effective.

PARAPHRASING

Paraphrasing is used when a client has expressed several thoughts or has unfolded a long story or a complicated incident. Paraphrasing allows the therapist to summarize what has been said, and to check that the client's statements have been heard correctly. It can be useful to clarify what the client has said by prefacing a question with 'It sounds like...' or 'Can I check that I have understood what you have been saying... It sounds like [this and that] has happened, and you are feeling... Have I understood this correctly?' This enables the client to disagree, or to clarify something further. Paraphrasing also helps the client to realize that the therapist is listening attentively to what is being said, and it helps the client slow down, or clarify what they are saying.

Paraphrasing is also used in music therapy to help the client and therapist develop a new theme within the session. It allows the therapist to recapitulate what has already occurred, and to make suggestions for what might follow. In the previous vignette, the music therapist used paraphrasing to remind Valerie that the song 'I did it my way' was her husband's favourite, and to then open up a conversation about him.

FOCUSED QUESTIONS AND PROBES TO ELICIT MORE INFORMATION

Combining open questions with reflections of the client's key words can help generate an accurate sense of how the person is feeling. The therapist might also use focused questions and probes to take the discussion further. For example, when a client describes what the music feels like, the therapist can ask more focused questions: 'I get a sense that this is an important feeling for you. Shall we explore this further?' is one way to move into a deeper, or more focused, exploration. Or the therapist might draw on knowledge of the client's history to probe further: 'I recall this was an issue with your family – you mentioned before that this is how you felt with your [mother/father]. Can we explore this further?' Another example might involve using an observation to suggest an issue: 'You seemed very uncomfortable and distracted when you were listening to that – was that music difficult for you?' Engaging at a deeper level depends on the therapist's experience, knowing what is appropriate and timely in the therapeutic process, and drawing on a deeper understanding and a secure relationship with the client.

Closure

At the end of the music therapy session, the therapist may provide closure by giving a summative description of what has happened in the session. They conclude by saying something about possibly seeing the person next time, or if another session is already scheduled, reminding the person of the next session.

Verbal interactions to enhance the experience of music

Paul Nolan (2005) also outlined the times we use verbal interactions to enhance the client's experiences in music. Clients often do not have the vocabulary for describing the music, and music therapists need to provide guidance to help. Nolan identified how we need to dialogue with clients about their music experience to enhance awareness of the aesthetic aspects of the music, their own musical behaviours and inner experiences, and interpersonal processes.

Therapists also listen attentively to the musical qualities of the client's voice. Elizabeth Schwartz suggests we 'listen to the musical qualities infused in [our] client's words and language to "hear" implicit or unconscious meanings and messages' (2019, p.63). She specifically mentions the melodic inflections, range of pitches, whether the dynamics are incongruent or the tempo pressured, as well as any unusual articulation or phrasing.

These musical cues can help therapists determine how to follow up with a client about their experience.

In the next chapter we focus more on the readiness of the participant for receptive experiences in music. This builds on the ideas in this chapter, and focuses on the specific affordances of music listening.

Chapter 2

Therapist-Selected Music for Receptive Methods

As we will describe throughout this book, there are many decision-making moments in music therapy practice that determine what you will do with different individuals and groups of people. Sometimes you will decide that it is most appropriate for you to take responsibility for the selection of music and how it will be used. Other times it will be more appropriate to collaborate with people to decide whether they are ready for a receptive music therapy experience, what music might be most appropriate, and whether it is appropriate to provide the experience in that context at that moment.

In this chapter we will provide some foundational ideas for those therapeutic encounters that require you to make decisions based on your expert knowledge of the diverse repertoire used in music therapy. This will include a set of selection principles to guide your thinking about which piece of music might be most suitable.

Throughout the chapter we focus on selection principles that can be applied to diverse genres. This means considering the musical characteristics, the complexity, how evocative the music is, its length and whether it invites meaning-making. Instrumental music, for example, may invite extra-musical meaning-making more readily than music with recognizable lyrics and more repetitively structured forms. We will consider the choice of pre-existing recorded music (instrumental and vocal) that is used in receptive music therapy sessions, such as intentional or focused listening, relaxation with music, and MI experiences. While it is ideal in music therapy to work collaboratively with people to choose music they would like to listen to, there are many situations when the therapist needs to take responsibility for making musical choices, and there are many conditions when this may be appropriate:

- The person is too young to make a choice (infants and young children).
- The person is too ill or confused to make a choice (adults with severe mental illness, those living with dementia or traumatic brain injury, non-verbal people with learning disabilities and disorders).
- The person is too tired and cannot decide between two or more selections of music (in palliative care, or a person undergoing treatment).
- Time is short – for example, the end of the session – when there isn't enough time to collaborate with the person.
- It is a group session, when making a collaborative choice would take a long time.

There are other good reasons to take responsibility for choosing the music for receptive music therapy experiences. In the remainder of this chapter we will focus on choosing instrumental music for receptive experiences such as focused listening, relaxation and MI.

ELEMENTS OF THE MUSIC

In choosing instrumental music for specific purposes the elements of the music are important considerations. The structure of music is multi-layered – there is (usually) a rhythmic foundation, a melodic line, a harmonic structure, the tone colour of the instruments and dynamic changes that enhance enjoyment and mood. These layers interweave and are often in parallel with each other, to create ever-changing layers of musical sound.

Some of the key music elements are:

- rhythm

- tempo
- melody
- harmony
- dynamics
- instrumentation.

Table 2.1 sets out the elements of music relative to arousal, predictability and mood.

Table 2.1 Elements and properties of music

Musical element	Arousal	Predictability	Mood
Rhythm	The more complex the rhythms, the more arousing they are to the listener. The simpler and more repetitive, the more peaceful	Steady rhythms that rely on repetition of rhythmic patterns, or the return of recognizable motifs, enhance predictability	Strong rhythms tend to drive a more determined mood, whereas gentle or arrhythmic patterns may allow for more imagination and floating
Tempo	Faster pace is usually associated with greater energy, whereas slower tempo is associated with calmness and reflection	Predictability is created through stable tempos that do not change dramatically between sections	A slower pace often reflects a gentler or more melancholy mood, where a quick pace suggests more movement and spirit
Melody	Melodies with wide leaps between notes demand attention, whereas melodies with small intervals are more calming	Singable melodies that are easy to recall and go in the direction that is expected create a sense of security	Melodies are often connected to memories and associations and afford projections and transferences of different meanings and moods onto the music

cont.

Musical element	Arousal	Predictability	Mood
Harmony	More complex harmonic patterns require greater attention and therefore higher engagement and arousal	More predictable harmonic progressions allow the listener to be carried without high cognitive demands	A music piece written in a minor key is often thought to suggest a sad, melancholic or reflective mood, but this is not always so. Similarly, a major key may not always sound happy
Dynamics	The more dramatic the dynamics, the more arousing they are, with greater movement encouraging higher levels of awareness	Repetition of dynamic features can foster predictability, although dynamic changes add colour to the music	The dynamics can be stretched out in a long crescendo to create a climax in the music, which is often felt as an opening up of emotion in the listener. The more dramatic, the more emotionally provocative
Instrumentation	The timbres of brass and percussive instruments are associated with more active states, such as brass marching bands; strings and woodwinds are often associated with being more reflective	Passing different sounds between instruments is a common compositional technique that enables repetition without monotony, whereas sudden changes defy prediction	Everyone has preferences for different timbres and often associate different moods with different sounds – from reedy oboes to high-pitched strings or deep bass sounds

ASSESSING THE COMPLEXITY OF THE MUSIC

Another way to reflect on whether a selection of music is appropriate for a receptive experience is to assess its intensity and complexity. Lars Ole Bonde (2005, p.358) was the first to distinguish 'supportive', 'challenging' and 'mixed' categories of music in relation to graphing the intensity profiles of music. These three categories were expanded by Margareta Wärja to form a taxonomy of therapeutic music that she found helpful in her korta musikresor (KMR) method (meaning 'short music journeys') (Wärja 2015).

Wärja and Bonde (2014, pp.18–19) outline this taxonomy as follows:

- *Supportive music* is used to create a safe framework around the music-listening experience. It can be (a) a secure and holding field, (b) a secure and opening field, or (c) a secure and exploratory field. It is stable, fairly predictable and stays within the mood spectrum of light moods. The music form can be simple ABA, ostinato-based, and in duple or ternary form. An example is *Secret Garden*: Papillon.

- *Mixed supportive and challenging music* has a supportive beginning and ending. However, some episodes may present the participant with challenges, by changing mood, tempo or volume, and a higher level of tension, which also means an increase in intensity. It can be (a) explorative with surprises and contrasts; (b) exploratory and deepening; or (c) explorative and challenging. The music form is more elaborate with contrasting sections, or rhapsodic. Examples are Elgar: *Sospiri*; Rodrigo: *Concierto de Aranjuez*, 2nd movement.

- *Challenging music* is highly intense. It can be powerful and dramatic, but also sustained in a certain mood and invite the participant to confront problems or explore emotional dilemmas or losses. The three fields of challenging music are: (a) the rhapsodic field; (b) the field of metamorphosis; and (c) the field of mystery and transformation. The music form is more complex, with contrasts in many music elements. Examples are Copland: *Appalachian Spring*; Barber: *Adagio for Strings*.

PREFERENCES FOR MUSIC GENRES

It is generally accepted that when choosing music for clients, the best fit is their preferred music. Ascertaining the preferred genre can be difficult because there are so many genres of music. 'Popular' music often means current songs, but if we are looking for preferred instrumental music to listen to, relax to or to generate imagery, we need to have a conversation about a broader spectrum of music preferences. Playing short examples of two or three selections and asking the person to choose can be one way to proceed, but sometimes our clients can't make a choice.

A wide diversity of music genres exists, and new ones are always emerging. The main genres used in receptive music therapy are:

- ambient/environmental and film music
- classical art music of the European tradition (that is, classical instrumental and vocal)
- world music
- contemporary youth music (hip-hop, pop, K-pop).

Ambient/environmental and film music

While it is difficult to generalize across a genre when describing its features, ambient music is, on the whole, 'easy to listen to' in that it requires little cognitive processing and there are no demands on the listener to make sense of the music or what it is about – it is simply pleasant to listen to. It falls under the 'supportive' framework in Wärja and Bonde's (2014) taxonomy. 'Easy listening' suggests the music style is familiar in form, meaning it has a predictable melody that is 'singable', an uncomplicated harmonic structure and a consistent bass line that holds the music securely. It is likely that the music is played on guitar, strings, mellow piano, flute or another pleasing timbre, and it is sometimes synthesized.

Some contemporary examples of ambient music include Enya, Daniel Kobialka and pianist Ludovico Einaudi.

AMBIENT/ENVIRONMENTAL MUSIC

Sounds of nature can evoke pleasant, relaxing and calming feelings, and can be coupled with supportive imagery – for example, 'imagining a scene in nature, the green of the trees, perhaps there is a waterfall nearby' – to encourage the person to bring these images to their mind. Sounds of the ocean may also be pleasant if the water is 'lapping' against the shore.

In contrast, it is important to note that environmental sounds can sometimes be confusing. For example, bird calls can be heard literally, as if there are birds in the room. This may be disconcerting for people who are living with dementia or who are not able to process the complexity of these experiences.

FILM MUSIC

Film music tends to be evocative of scenes being played out on the screen. Most people would recognize the *Superman* theme, music from *Star Wars*, or the themes from *Harry Potter* and *The Lord of the Rings*. Often these themes are well known because the film has been watched many times. When selecting music for therapeutic purposes, it is important to consider these kinds of existing associations with the music selection, for example associations that arise not only in memories of the film, but also by identification with characters in the story. This can be discussed with the person or group prior to listening, or afterwards, if necessary.

Aaron Copland (1953, p.205) suggests several ways in which music 'serves the screen'. These include both background and foreground roles, such as underlining unspoken thoughts and unseen implications, as well as building a sense of continuity across time, and more predictably, by contributing to the creation of atmosphere, 'underpinning the theatrical build-up of a scene and rounding it off with a sense of finality' (Copland 1953, pp.205–206).

These purposes are experienced powerfully in John Williams' scores for *Star Wars*. Some are inspiring of hope, love and the triumph of good over evil. Others depict sadness and betrayal. The structure of the main theme in each of these is a long ascending line that immediately lifts the audience's mood and excites and inspires. Williams uses his themes like leitmotifs, bringing in fragments of the theme to remind the viewer of key characteristics of the actor's role, and to give an emotional sense of what the character is feeling. He also uses massed voices (like a choir) to suggest something beyond the normal.

Williams also wrote the film score for *Schindler's List*, a story that is harrowing in places, conveyed using music to depict a diversity of emotions. The main theme in this film is played by violinist Isaac Stern, and conveys the anguish of the story through a haunting melody, comprising falling intervals of fifths and sixths in a minor key.

Classical art music of the European tradition

The term 'classical' music can be problematic in discussing different genres of music since it covers a multitude of composers and stylistic periods, from the Baroque (1600–1750) to the present day. It can be confused with the 'classical' era of European music (approximately 1750–1820). The music of the Impressionists (1890–1925, including Debussy, Ravel, Fauré, Respighi and others) falls under the genre 'classical', yet the music is in stark contrast to the formal structures of music from the Baroque and Classic period. Each era of European classical music can be used therapeutically, particularly with adult recipients, depending on the intention of the session.

Helen Bonny, who founded the Guided Imagery and Music (GIM) method that now bears her name (Bonny Method of GIM), has written extensively about the features of classical music (2002, pp.301–324). She articulates several beliefs about music from this tradition:

- Classical Western music has stood the test of time, and is as relevant today as in past centuries.
- Music from this tradition provides for the building up of tension and subsequent release in the flow and unfolding progression of the music over time. The release can be felt as cathartic.
- There is a formal structure to music of the classic tradition, and that structure helps to contain the emotional experience of the listener. A small container is one where the music is predictable, there is repetition and it has clear boundaries. A large container is one where the music is unpredictable, where there may be large

changes in the dynamics that require the listener to regulate emotionally so they are not flooded by the experience.

- There is a flow to classical music that underpins the flow of imagery and emotions. Melody, harmony, the timbre of the instruments and changing dynamics add to the way the music extends over time. This layering of the music contributes to stimulating imagery and changes in mood.
- Classical music offers variability in the stimulus. For example, it is common to have a major theme, followed by a contrasting softer theme (often in a minor key) to evoke differing moods.
- Classical music conveys mood through a combination of factors – the melodic line, the sequence of harmonies, the timbre of the instruments, and dynamics of crescendo and diminuendo. In addition, the listener may have associations with the style of music that can activate memories.

Many of these characteristics also apply to other music genres, although classical music is particularly structured in a way that enables tension and release, which stimulates flow and movement, and creates or sustains mood over a longer period than other genres.

MINIMALISM

A contemporary advancement in European classical music is minimalism. As the title suggests, its key feature is repetition of one of the elements in a simple form (Hanning 2002). Exponents of minimalism are Steve Reich, Philip Glass, Estonian composer Arvo Pärt and Max Richter. One of Pärt's compositions that is used frequently in receptive music therapy is *Spiegel im Spiegel*, meaning 'Mirror(s) in the mirror'. The solo instrument is a cello or viola, accompanied by the piano. The structure of the music is circular, capturing the cyclic experience of observing mirrors within mirrors. The tempo is slow (about 72 beats per minute [bpm]), and the timbre of the solo instrument is deep and full sounding, with long held notes. The piano accompaniment features broken chords in the upper part, and gentle octaves in the lower part, to keep the music 'grounded'.

World music

Having discussed classical art music of the European tradition, we also acknowledge the traditional art music of other cultures. Wai Man Ng (2015, 2018) has written extensively about the music of the Chinese culture, and how this is used effectively in evoking imagery of Chinese archetypal symbols and scenery. Traditional Chinese music dates back 5000 years, and, as with all genres of music, newer forms have a blend of traditional Chinese with Western elements, particularly Western harmonies. Although Ng developed five Chinese programmes to be used in GIM, some of the individual selections can be used for other purposes.

Although it is impossible to summarize the extensive and ancient traditions of music in different cultures, there is some value in highlighting specific aspects of some that are often used in receptive music therapy in the West. For example, the ragas of Indian culture that are used at specific times of the day have special meaning. The raga is a series of notes played in a fixed ascending and descending order, in keeping with the mood it represents, and it can instil deep states of consciousness (Clark and Kini 2011, p.140). Likewise, the modal scales of Middle Eastern music date back thousands of years, and the music has a distinctive sound due to the tonal system being based in the Aeolian mode. The instruments of the Middle East are the oud (a pear-shaped instrument), saz (a long necked lute) and qanun (a stringed instrument).

Contemporary music

There are many instrumental tracks that could also be drawn from contemporary pop music for use in receptive music therapy. Both electronic and acoustic music have been composed that contain many of the features described in Table 2.1, such as long melodic lines, predictable structures, prominent bass lines and repetitive harmonic frameworks. Although the features are the same, the sound is very different, and may be preferred by some people, both young people and those who prefer more contemporary sounds, or those who don't like the orchestral sounds that typify the other genres.

Electronic dance music (EDM) is one super-genre, consisting of at least 300 sub-genres (McLeod 2001). Repetitive beats are a feature of EDM, with the presence of a consistent, 4/4 rhythm that is often between 120 and 180 bpm (Cannon and Greasley 2021). EDM is distinguished from hip-hop because of its lack of emphasis on words, and it is usually without lyrics. Many people find EDM peaceful because of these musical features, which lend themselves to predictability and a sense of containment.

Since there is a vast amount of contemporary music, it can be difficult to identify particular tracks that will suit the purpose of a receptive music therapy experience. This task has been made simpler by the creation of digital music streaming services with inbuilt search engines. Keywords can be used to identify a sub-set of songs that you can listen to and decide which ones will be useful. Table 2.2 contains some examples of useful search terms that might aid in thinking about how to search for music for a specific purpose. Searches like these will often result in findings that include playlists created by other listeners where you might discover an array of sounds with keywords associated. These will all need to be checked for purpose, but provide an excellent and stimulating beginning.

Table 2.2 Music style and keywords

Music style	Keywords
Electronic dance music (EDM)	Relax, chill out, weekend vibes
Trance music	Relax, beach, chill, Zen
Popular music, instrumental	Peaceful, meditation, relaxed, background, soothing
Jazz, instrumental	Croon, soft, coffee, chill, cool

ASSESSING A MUSIC SELECTION FOR SUITABILITY

It is advisable to always listen to the music selection yourself before using it with clients, and to listen to it both subjectively and objectively (Copland 1953, p.15). It is important to listen to the selection under three different conditions:

- Condition 1: Listen with your eyes closed and with full attention on the music selection – do not have the music playing in the background while attending to other things such as driving the car or cooking dinner. Be fully attentive to the music. Listen for the various elements – rhythm, melody, harmonic progressions and instrumentation – and mentally evaluate whether these elements together create the effect you want.

- Condition 2: Listen to the selection again, imagining what type of images or feelings might be aroused in the client/client group with whom you intend to use it. Be particularly careful about whether the selection is likely to engender sad or depressed feelings, as many relaxation tracks are written in a minor key, have a descending melodic line, and can easily be depressing for clients who might be in a vulnerable state in hospital or in an aged care facility, for example.
- Condition 3: Listen carefully to the beginning of the selection and to the ending. Does the beginning create the atmosphere that you want? Or is there a lengthy introduction before the section that you really want to use begins? Is the ending of the music well grounded, or does the music leave the client with a floating ending that might make it difficult for them to feel that the music has finished?

It is important to keep a note of what selections work well and which do not with individuals and groups. This facilitates a self-education process and enables therapists to build their own repertoire of music selections that are certain to achieve what is desired.

CHOOSING THE MUSIC FOR INDIVIDUAL SESSIONS

Rationale for *expert* choice-making

The therapist (the expert) may choose the music under various conditions, relative to the age of the client/patient, and the physical or cognitive limitations of that person. One advantage of expert-chosen music is that the therapist has an understanding and knowledge of the elements of music that might underpin the decision, for example, the tempo of the music, whether it is written in a major or minor key, or the predominant mood of the music.

Young children have the capacity to listen attentively to music and to create stories of imagination (Reher 2015). Due to the child's age, the therapist generally chooses the music, as they have the expert knowledge of genres and styles that might suit and support the child. It is possible that the child may have preferences for music, and where possible, the therapist will include the child in a collaborative decision.

In aged care, particularly where the person has dementia, the therapist (expert) chooses the music based on knowledge of the music likely to be preferred by the client. We know that music preferences are established during the adolescent years (North, Hargreaves and O'Neill 2000), and a therapist can calculate the likely preferences of an older adult by their age. Although this is an imperfect tool, it can be a good starting point. Over time, therapists may also gather information about preferred music from sessions focused on music listening.

Expert-chosen music is also indicated when the client has a physical condition that may impact their ability to make choices, such as where the client may be physically tired and in pain and, when given a choice, they may be overwhelmed by that simple request. Similarly, patients who have sustained a traumatic brain injury may have cognitive impairment that could restrict their ability to make a decisive choice about their preferred music. The therapist may also choose the music for a person with severe mental illness where cognition is impacted and the person may have difficulty choosing one song/selection over another.

Rationale for *collaborative* choice-making

A collaborative process in choosing music empowers the participant to be engaged in decision-making about music listening, and to begin to develop their own expertise. By focusing on music that is the best fit for how the participant is feeling at the time, the therapist can guide the choice in a way that enables discussion of healthy versus unhealthy music for the participant. This involves identifying music that matches and mirrors the participant's mood, different music for times when they want to change their mood, and different choices again, when they want to connect with a particular state. This kind of discrimination in music choices is more nuanced than 'I like it/don't like it', and promotes more effective uses of music for times when that is useful. It also ensures that people are not dependent on a music therapist to guide them towards good music choices that serve a therapeutic or wellbeing purpose.

A collaborative process can also involve offering choices when the person is not able to initiate their own choice. This frequently happens when the client says, 'You choose' to the therapist. In this instance the therapist can scaffold the decision-making process by playing a short excerpt of two pieces and then ask the participant to choose between the two. This would be an appropriate process if the participant is withdrawn, depressed or physically or emotionally compromised. It is not demanding, but it still emphasizes the importance of agency, and gently moves the participant from passive listening towards more active involvement.

Rationale for *client* choice-making

One advantage of client choice-making is that the participant has an existing relationship with the music – it is known to them. It reflects their preferred genres and styles, and is therefore familiar and safe for them. In addition, when the participant chooses the music, they are asserting agency by making the choice. The therapist can become familiar with the participant's preferred playlists, and this can provide useful information for discussion. It can also enhance the therapeutic relationship and support the building of rapport between the therapist and participant because there is more reciprocity.

Since people who can initiate intentional choices are cognitively able to reflect and consider possibilities, the purpose of music listening in this context is usually to promote personal insights through discussion. Discussion will focus on the meaning of the song to the individual, rather than on new meanings that might be generated through imagination and sensorial imagery experiences.

The first step in this process is to find out about what music is important to the person. The therapist will typically ask informal questions, such as:

- What kind of music do you like to listen to when you're on your own?

- What music do you like to share with other people?
- What music do you listen to when you're feeling sad/angry/lost/lonely?
- What music do you listen to when you're trying to change your mood?

The next step is to listen together. The therapist needs to encourage focused listening during this process, since most people are used to having music on in the background and talking over the top of it. In order to encourage a commitment to music listening, sometimes the therapist may need to model listening, possibly by sitting back and staring into the distance rather than making eye contact, or holding a steady gaze at the floor or another spot. If the person talks, it is important to acknowledge them and explain what you are doing, with comments like 'Yes, that's interesting. I'm just focusing on listening to your music. Shall we listen together?' This avoids making interpretations or pushing the client to behave in a certain way, but makes clear the intentionality of music listening.

After the music has finished, the therapist will often begin with an open question probe to solicit what is most meaningful:

- So, what is it you like about that music?
- What stood out to you about listening to that music today?
- How was it to share that music?

The client will often assume that the therapist expects them to focus on the musical material and to describe the composer or the performers. This is a useful beginning point, but meaning-making requires movement beyond the more aesthetic domains and towards associations people have. This might connect with past experiences: 'I remember the first time I heard that/saw that/bought that.' It might also relate to memories of certain people or special events.

CHOOSING THE MUSIC FOR GROUP SESSIONS (EXPERT-CHOSEN)

Choosing music for group sessions requires skill, and a good knowledge of music that is 'middle-of-the-road', meaning that it is likely to be appreciated by most people in the group. This will depend on how diverse group members are, especially with regard to culture and age. For example, the age range within the group might vary across several decades. A group of carers of people living with dementia, for example, may include a spouse or a daughter or son of the person living with dementia. The age range might be from 40 to 90, and the choice of music needs to sit comfortably with all of them, as far as possible.

Factors to consider in making a choice are:

- time available for the group to listen and process
- the age range of the group, which might indicate which genre of music to choose
- the prevailing mood of the group
- the intention of the listening activity
- group dynamics.

Another important part of decision-making is related to time constraints. Normally, it is important to allow time for people to reflect on the receptive experience and to verbalize how they felt during the listening. Intention is an important factor in considering how much time is needed, and therefore how long the piece of music can be. It is important to consider things such as: is the receptive experience choosing a song with discussion, or relaxation designed to wrap up the session, or will it be the main method of the whole session? If a receptive experience comes at the end of a music therapy group, you may only have 2–3 minutes for the music, with a short period of time for discussion, and this will override any lengthy discussion about genre and preferences. All these factors and more will play into the decision.

The prevailing mood of the group is another key factor in choosing music for listening. If the mood is predominantly withdrawn and depressed, a suitable music selection would be one that invites reflection to match the energy level of the group. If the prevailing mood is bright and energetic, the chosen music may be in a major key, with stimulating instrumentation.

The intention of the listening activity depends on the depth of reflection that seems feasible for the members and to what degree in-depth conversations are beneficial to them. The group of carers of people living with dementia may be pitched at 'easy' listening, whereas a group of cancer survivors might require music of some depth that speaks to the complexity of the cancer journey.

Group dynamics is another factor to consider in the choice-making decision. Where the dynamics are complicated by a dominant member of the group, the choice of music might be best placed somewhere along that person's preferences, to enable the listening activity to proceed. However, some groups may be set up to address dynamics such as a person dominating the group. In this instance a collaborative approach may be instituted where the therapist plays the beginning of two possibilities and then chooses the one most people prefer. This would intentionally bring challenging dynamics to the fore so they can be processed.

In the following chapter we will describe another key consideration for determining the focus, depth and decision-making within therapy. The readiness of the individual or group to use music in deeper or gentler ways is important to consider. Some might argue that it is the most important consideration for focused music listening.

Chapter 3

Focused Music Listening

'Focused music listening' describes a directed and engaged approach to listening that requires active attention. The creative artist and performer of Indian classical music Ansuman Biswas emphasizes how this is a skill that requires practice, with deeper listening resulting in greater appreciation (2011, pp.102–103). The American musician Aaron Copland (1900–90) similarly suggested that music listening is sensuous, expressive and pleasurable, and both subjective and objective; and ultimately, he emphasized that we are 'listening *for* something' (1953, p.15).

In this chapter we address focused listening to music, sometimes referred to as 'intentional listening' or 'deep listening'. A starting point is to assess the readiness of the participant to listen intentionally.

READINESS OF THE RECIPIENT

A person's readiness to participate in a receptive music therapy experience is core to this text. Most dictionary definitions of being 'receptive' include reference to being willing, responsive, open, admitting and/or prepared to consider:

- Cambridge Dictionary: 'Willing to listen to and accept new ideas and suggestions'
- Merriam-Webster: 'Open and responsive to ideas, impressions, or suggestions'
- Dictionary.com: 'Having the quality of receiving, taking in, or admitting'

- Collins: 'Someone who is receptive to new ideas or suggestions and is prepared to consider them or accept them'
- Macmillan: 'Willing to listen or to consider suggestions'.

Being receptive is multi-dimensional in music therapy, since the individual needs to be open to both the music and a relationship with their therapist. People vary considerably in their ability to trust both, based on their life experiences, their personal tendencies and the context in which the therapeutic relationship is occurring. We propose four dimensions that require careful consideration in identifying what depth of receptive music therapy might be feasible for an individual, which are now described in detail:

- the person's existing relationship with music
- their willingness to listen intentionally
- their capacity for emotional regulation
- their arousal.

UNDERSTANDING PEOPLE'S EXISTING RELATIONSHIP WITH MUSIC

An important part of the initial introduction to music therapy is learning about the nature of a person's existing relationship with music. Randi Rolvsjord (2010) describes this relationship as a resource that people bring to music therapy that can be appropriated for the purposes of therapy. This can be true, although it is also possible that people have developed unhelpful relationships with music (McFerran and Saarikallio 2013) that need to be considered before suggesting what type of receptive music therapy experience should be used. For example, people may have developed a habit of depending on music to make them feel better in a way that sublimates their own agency into the object that is music. Or they may be using music to intensify negative emotions such as sadness or anger without the ability to benefit from the release of emotion to feel better afterwards. They might be using music to isolate themselves from others by identifying with the persona of an artist and rejecting the human relationships available in their relational field.

Some tools have been developed to assess a person's relationship with music, including the Healthy–Unhealthy Music Scale (HUMS) (Saarikallio *et al.* 2015) and the Interest in Music tool (Gold *et al.* 2013). However, the most straightforward way to do this is to talk with the person about their music preferences and to embed questions about the nature of their relationship with music in that discussion, along with discovering their aesthetic preferences. This serves the development of the therapeutic relationship at the same time as discovering more about their existing music listening habits, which can be used to decide what to do next.

The kinds of questions that can be useful to prompt reflections by people about the nature of their existing relationship with music include the following.

To identify rumination:

- Is that song associated with particular experiences you have had? Do you think about them often?
- Does it feel useful to reconnect with those associations in a way that is always the same?
- Does it feel like a ritual for you?

To identify intensification:

- How do you feel after listening to songs that are about sadness/rage/loneliness?
- Does your mood change from before to after music listening? Is it in the way you had hoped for?
- Do you choose that song because you hope it will make you feel better? Does it work?

To identify isolation:

- Do you prefer listening to music to being with family and friends? Why is that?

- Do you have any people in your networks that understand you as well as the artists seem to?
- Does it feel repetitive that they always say/sing the same thing?

Your role is to support people in developing ways of listening to music that support their health and wellbeing. However, it would be naïve to assume that music always has a positive influence in people's lives. People use music in the same ways that they use shopping and exercise, food and alcohol, substances, and work. They can be abused, or they can be leveraged as a resource. Music has no inherent energy or positive force of its own. It is something that people may utilize for coping in ways that reflect their inner patterns. Our role is to identify any uses of music listening for coping that are unhelpful and to foster uses that are helpful.

It is also critical therefore to recognize that no types of music are more helpful than others. Richard Wagner can be used to inspire or depress. Metal music can activate positive energy or negative. Country music can be validating or deflating. Music therapists, more than any other professionals, should be aware that the tendency to label types of music as causing responses is a flawed notion. This is why our profession involves subjectively assessing people's existing relationship with music, not objectively diagnosing them based on their music preferences. If it were that easy, we would be able to heal the world by prescribing a type of music that would alleviate its problems with violence and injustice and unfair privilege. If only that was possible.

ENCOURAGING PEOPLE'S WILLINGNESS TO LISTEN INTENTIONALLY

Another part of understanding a person's readiness for different levels of receptive music therapy focuses on their willingness to listen with purpose. Many people have strong relationships with music, but they do not always want to use that relationship within the therapeutic realm. Perhaps their relationship with music is exactly as they want it to be, and they do not want to risk connecting it with the issues that led them to therapy. Libby Flynn, a music therapy researcher, has shown that people's relationships with music are precious and that music therapy can change existing associations and replace them with new ones (2014). Sometimes, this is a very positive outcome, such as when people have been using music to ruminate on a failed relationship and they decide to use a different song as an empowerment anthem instead. Or they might choose to change the meaning of a favourite song so that it becomes more positive. One young man did this by repeatedly playing his preferred songs whenever he had a positive social experience, instead of listening to them when he was feeling down and seeking comfort. Through intentionally changing the times he was listening to his favourite tracks, he began to use them to lift his mood, rather than reinforcing a negative state. However, there were people in Flynn's research who found their preferred songs more painful after using them in therapy because they had taken on meanings and associations with their grief when previously they had been songs of pleasure. This is just one example that illustrates why people need to choose whether they are willing to use music listening as part of their therapy.

Once the person has given informed consent to use their relationship with music, the purpose needs to be agreed on. Therapy is only as effective as the individual or group is willing for it to be – it requires an intention to benefit (Duncan, Miller and Sparks 2004). In receptive music therapy, this intention expands beyond a commitment to the therapeutic relationship as the vessel for growth, because it also encompasses music listening as an equally powerful force. This is based on the belief that music is not just a tool in therapy, but also functions as a co-therapist, inviting another layer of opportunity for growth. It is part of the therapeutic belief system, which requires this intentional commitment to the process and purpose of therapy be made, and in receptive music therapy, intentional music listening is a powerful part of that.

Music therapist Katarina Mårtenson Blom (2011) describes the importance of developing a shared intention for the music listening experience in therapy. She describes how the therapist and recipient must share both *intention* and *attention* for the purposes of therapy, and this combination enables a form of surrender to what solutions the music might offer. Her research was focused specifically on Guided Imagery and Music (GIM), which can be considered a very deep level of both listening and therapy.

However, the notion of surrender is found throughout the psychotherapy literature and has relevance to a range of receptive music therapy experiences.

Mårtenson Blom associates the ability to surrender to the music as opening possibilities for transcendence, in contrast to the notion of submission, which is the sometimes somewhat gendered association people often make with surrender. She quotes Emmanuel Ghent:

> To experience surrender is to experience being in the moment, totally in the present, where past and future, the two tenses that require 'mind' in the sense of secondary processes, have receded from consciousness. Its ultimate direction is the discovery of one's identity, one's sense of self, one's sense of wholeness, even one's sense of unity with other living beings. This is quite unlike submission... (Ghent 1990, p.216, cited in Mårtenson Blom 2011, p.187)

The emphasis on attention is clear in this quote, and part of the surrender to receptive music therapy is being able to focus on the music. This involves several elements, such as the cognitive ability to listen without being more than normally distracted. Although attending to and following elements of music takes training, many non-musicians have trained themselves to be excellent music listeners through hours of practice. These people find focusing on the music relatively easy, and the focus of the therapeutic conversation is on the purpose of this listening. Music listening has been described as one of the ways to achieve flow for this reason (Csikszentmihalyi 2002).

For those who have not practised listening carefully to music, it is important to spend time working on this capacity. Music therapist Susanna Scott-Moncrieff highlights the value of repeated listening early in the therapeutic process to develop the capacity for listening deeply (Scott-Moncrieff, Beck and Montgomery 2015). She suggests using prompts during music listening to help people to stay focused, and makes specific suggestions about allowing yourself to enjoy the music, or taking your time, noticing everything as you listen deeply, and even listening more deeply (Scott-Moncrieff 2019).

Lisa Summer's (2009) investigations of how clients experienced the music in GIM suggested that 'repeated music and music-centered verbal guiding created a receptive listening attitude in the client and deepened the client's relational capacity toward the music' (2009, p.60). This can be seen as a way of practising or preparing to listen intentionally to the music as a part of receptive music therapy experiences. It helps to clarify that it is necessary to really listen, and that the act of doing so can lead to the discovery of answers that are otherwise difficult to retrieve from within the person's own knowing.

EMOTIONAL REGULATION

It is not only sharing attention and intention that is necessary for a receptive music therapy experience to be meaningful. Katarina Mårtenson Blom (2011) notes a third dimension that is more emotional and involves sharing affect and attunement within the therapeutic alliance. Emotional readiness once again relates to both the music and the therapist, since both can trigger strong emotional responses, and together, this is intensified and worthy of careful consideration.

Jennifer Bibb, a music therapist who often plays songs with groups of adults in mental health recovery, discovered that many members would have strong emotional reactions to songs that were suggested by people in the group (Bibb and McFerran 2018). They described being 'triggered' by certain songs and needing to manage their emotional reactions. To do this, they drew on their trust in the music therapist and the belief that she would be able to contain them if it was necessary. They also talked about needing to develop skills in self-regulating, and believing that the positive context of the group provided them with opportunities to practise doing so. The group was not the only place where music triggered a reaction in them, and there were other things beyond music that had the same effect. Therefore, although they didn't describe wanting to be protected from the emotional power of the music, it is important for music therapists to know that many were having internal reactions that were not always obvious even to an attentive observer.

This might be an important distinction between group and individual therapy, since we would expect to be able to verbally process a strong affective reaction to music in an individual session. Nonetheless, receptive music therapy experiences do emphasize the value of internal relationships and private reactions to music. Perhaps this happens more often than during active music therapy experiences where the sharing is embodied and expressed in ways that are more palpable. Therefore, our ability as therapists to understand how well people can regulate their own emotions is important to ensure client safety.

Many people assume that music listening is safer than more overtly expressive forms of music therapy. There are numerous studies in the literature that describe nurses using music in hospitals, for example, as one of the many tasks they will attend to within their busy schedule. Sometimes interventions that use music listening without a therapist are found to be effective, as seen in the Cochrane Reviews of music and pain (Cepeda *et al.* 2006). Therefore, it is not necessary to assume that all wellbeing interventions that use music listening are dangerous. However, it is important to consider which people might be more vulnerable than others to being triggered, and people who have had adverse life experiences should be carefully considered.

The literature on trauma emphasizes safety, and this is a fundamental component of Judith Herman's (1992) ground-breaking work on trauma and recovery. This is because people who have had adverse experiences have also experienced damage to their ability to trust. Acts that may seem simple to some people in receptive music therapy may be exceedingly difficult for others. Consider how challenging it might be to close your eyes and surrender to the music if your ability to trust others has been damaged. Therefore, it is essential to avoid assumptions about what will be the 'easy' parts of the experience, and to step carefully towards any encounter that assumes safety.

It is not only the trusting relationship offered by the therapist that some clients need to be wary of; it is also their ability to trust how they will react to the music. One aspect of this is the triggering described in Jennifer Bibb's study (Bibb and McFerran 2018), which was related to pre-existing associations that people might have with music that they did not expect to hear. However, even unfamiliar music can provoke a strong emotional reaction since there are so many simultaneous points of possibility within music, which is why it provides such a rich tapestry for therapeutic work. But the sound of an instrument, a particular type of climax, a sudden change in direction or a contrast of dynamics can all be startling for a person whose fundamental ability to react calmly has been damaged.

These strong emotional affordances are the reason that music is considered to have such value in therapy. Alf Gabrielsson's (2011) work has detailed a long list of strong experiences with music that people commonly describe, including a number that are related to feelings and emotions. These include strong, intense feelings, positive feelings and negative feelings, as well as mixed, contradictory and changed feelings. These emotional experiences can be extremely helpful. They can also be frightening or unsettling. If a vulnerable person spends a lot of time trying to regulate their emotional state, the unexpected emotions that are provoked by music can be disturbing.

Once again, it is not necessary to protect people from their own emotions. People will often know when they need to play it safe, and they will quickly describe their concerns, or flatly reject the idea of engaging with music in therapy. These responses should not be assumed to be defensive or resistive. They may be well informed, and the decision to avoid music as a strategy for emotion regulation can be an indicator of excellent self-knowing. However, most people do not need to avoid music altogether. What they need is a therapist who is attentive to their concerns, respectful of what they need, aware of how music can provoke a range of strong emotions, and careful about staging experiences appropriately to be safe.

AROUSAL

Another response that people can have to music in the context of therapy is related to their level of arousal. This topic has once again been prominent in the discourse on trauma because it is another area of the self that can be damaged through adverse and stressful experiences, as well as a range of medical conditions and cognitive differences. The power of music to arouse people is not simply a reference to emotions; it is a broader notion that encompasses energy levels and is often used to refer to an optimal state of functioning.

One way that arousal has been described is through the construct of the 'window of tolerance', initially introduced through the work of Dan Siegel (1999). This is as an ideal state for receptive music therapy experiences, where the individual is neither over (hyper) nor under (hypo) aroused. When over-aroused, a traumatized person might be hyper-vigilant and feel anxious, and so music could be used to help calm them and return them to a state of balance where therapeutic work can occur. Mindfulness-based interventions have been recommended in these situations, as examined by Patricia Ogden (Ogden, Minton and Pain 2006), and music listening has also been recommended. Several studies using quantitative data have found music listening to be effective in work with those who have post-traumatic stress disorder (PTSD), influencing physiological regulation and resulting in improved sleep, increased relaxation and the reduction of negative PTSD symptoms (Beck *et al.* 2018; Bensimon, Bodner and Shrira 2017; Jespersen and Vuust 2012; Rudstam *et al.* 2017).

At the other end of the spectrum, some people may become non-reactive as a way of coping with stress. In the case of trauma, this can result in emotional numbness or even paralysis in the most extreme cases, such as those reported in Sigmund Freud's early case studies (1966). In other contexts, stress or illness can result in a lack of motivation and challenges in getting out of bed, leaving the house, engaging in meaningful activities, and connecting with friends and family. Here, music can be used as a stimulus to support people in acting, and to motivate them into a more optimal state, where more insight-oriented work can occur.

Although the 'window of tolerance' is a useful notion for understanding when people are dysregulated, we do not suggest that people must be in an optimal state before they participate in receptive music therapy experiences. This would result in a privileged few having access to the many helpful affordances of music. Rather, it is critical that the music therapist considers what the client's state of arousal is, and how receptive music therapy experiences could be used to motivate, calm or engage in deep therapeutic work. This will depend on the person, the context, the day and the hour, and can fluctuate even more often. Since music can influence arousal, we always need to be sensitive to how this is happening. Not only do we consider what the person might need, but we also carefully observe how they are reacting throughout the receptive music therapy experience. We watch their face, their breathing, their body movements, their eyes, as well as seeking verbal clarification where necessary. And then we adjust to ensure the optimal therapeutic experience for that person at that moment in time.

INTENTIONAL LISTENING

One of the first music therapists to research intentional listening was Lisa Summer who developed the idea of 'music-centred guiding' (2009). Her approach involved asking participants to listen to one piece of music repeatedly, during which she used music-centred guiding to establish the music as the primary therapeutic agent (Summer 2009, p.3). She found that the four music therapist participants were able to use this process of deep listening to listen more deeply to their internal world. In a post-session they produced rich descriptions of their music experience that showed a successive change in listening attitude, and hence a changed relational capacity towards the music that deepened during the music programme.

Intentional listening also underpins Summer's Continuum Model of music and imagery (2012, 2019). This incorporates a three-tiered approach (drawn from Wheeler's 1983 model for music therapy) as a basis for the three levels of practice:

- supportive MI: resource-oriented, with repeated supportive music that is simple with little tension and no structural development
- re-educative MI: issue-oriented, with repeated music matching the issue being used that is again simple and repetitive, but has some tension and structural development
- re-constructive MI: transformative-oriented, with evocative and complex music that has significant structural development.

Drawing on Summer's model, Susanna Scott-Moncrieff has developed a Decision Tree process that offers various options for the different levels of music listening within therapy. The Decision Tree is based on a series of parameters that determine the decision. For example, one of the primary questions is whether the participant can emotionally regulate. If

- Is it hard to stop listening to music that connects you to bad memories?
- When you try to use music to feel better, do you ever end up feeling worse?
- Does music help you block people out?
- Do you like to listen to songs over and over, even though it makes you feel worse?
- Does music ever make you feel bad about yourself?
- Do you use music as an excuse not to face up to the real world?
- Does music ever help you to do things you shouldn't do?

These questions are focused on the unhelpful ways that people can use music. It would not be useful to run through these questions in a list, because people would not be likely to disclose their uses in a context that sounds judgemental and negative. In fact, most people are not aware of the ways that their music use is influencing them. They bring many positive assumptions about how helpful music has been to them throughout their lives – in feeling affirmed, understood, energized and connected. This is because these are the most common experiences with music. As music therapists, we are skilled in building on these pre-existing skills and encouraging people to develop further strategies that involve healthy uses of music in their everyday lives.

However, research has shown that people's musical identities change when they experience mental illness (Hense, McFerran and McGorry 2014). Cherry Hense introduced the idea of 'musical symptoms' to capture the changes young people described in their musical identity with their experience of acute mental illness. Musical symptoms aligned with aspects of young people's pathology and fed into illness behaviours of self-isolation – for example, depression sometimes resulted in more privatized musical symptoms, borderline personality disorder may be associated with more fragmented symptoms, and psychosis might lead to more disconnected musical symptoms.

Music therapists need to be aware of these changes in uses of music and musical expression because people generally are not. They assume that music will continue to play the same role it always has in their lives, and it often takes very careful, gentle questioning before they will even acknowledge that they are not getting the results they were expecting from musical listening. Being curious, not judgemental, about people's uses of music is part of our professional identity, and is even more important as people's mental health changes.

In one study with adolescents (McFerran and Saarikallio 2013), we asked the young people about their music listening, and began with:

> Are there ever any times where you feel worse after listening to music?

The participants in the study almost always said, 'No', making statements like 'Music is my daily vitamin pill/saviour/best friend,' etc. We would acknowledge and validate what a powerful source of support music can be, before probing a little more.

> Oh yes. Can you give me an example of one time where music helped you like that? What was happening? What music did you choose? Why did you choose that music? How did you feel afterwards?

Participants would then recount a story that demonstrated their helpful uses of music and explain why they thought of music as being so powerful. We would affirm this, and then probe again:

> So, I can see that music plays a really important role in your life. Many people we have spoken to say the same thing, but they can usually think of a time when music didn't bring them the results they were hoping for. Can you?

After some time for reflection, people would often come up with stories:

> Well, usually when I fight with my parents/partner I end up storming out of the house, and I take my music with me. I hope that if I listen to it as I walk, I will calm down and will be able to resolve the argument. But sometimes it does make me feel angrier, like it helps me justify my anger, so it doesn't get better.

> When my parents/neighbours are fighting, it drives me crazy. I get so frustrated listening to them. So, I go to my room and listen to music loud

> so that I don't have to hear them. But when the song is over, and they are still arguing, sometimes I use the energy I have built up to run screaming through the house, trying to get them to stop.
>
> When I broke up with my partner, there was one song we used to love and now I listen to that song over and over. It helps me stay connected to them, but it also makes me cry. It's been 18 months now and my best friend actually deleted the song off my phone last week, saying, 'Enough is enough!'

None of these examples is particularly problematic or surprising. However, it does help to highlight patterns of music use that are not helpful. They reflect music use for intensifying, ruminating and isolating. Once these examples have been bought into conscious awareness, people will often have an 'ah-hah' moment, where they recognize that music listening can be both helpful and unhelpful. This is the basis for more intentional selection of music, and it can help people to recognize that they shouldn't always just trust their instincts about choosing the right music. During difficult moments, they may need to be more conscious and intentional about their decision-making, which might involve asking themselves questions like 'How will this make me feel?' 'Is that what I want right now?'

VIGNETTE: Responsibility for music choice

Mary came to music therapy because she was struggling to feel positive about her life and wanted something to help her feel better. She loved music and would often play music loudly in the family home when she was trying to create a vibe or inspire domestic chores. Mary had been diagnosed with ADHD (attention-deficit hyperactivity disorder) as an adult and had difficulty organizing her home and following through from plans into action, which meant that she was constantly frustrated that her outer world was not what she hoped it to be. She had had some shocking and frightening experiences in the past that she found traumatic, and had spent a good deal of time in the past 10 years unable to get out of bed.

In Mary's case, the music therapist decided to take responsibility for choosing the music. Choice-making was a challenge for Mary, and it was not helpful to spend a lot of time empowering music-making decisions. The focus of the therapy was not on behavioural change and opportunities to rehearse more positive behaviours. Mary wanted to connect more deeply with her inner self and her reason for living, which she was disconnected from. Therefore, working with the unconscious barriers to her full flourishing was the intention of therapy, and the music therapist was best placed to use her expertise to choose music for that purpose on a given day. In addition, this freed Mary to focus on herself and her inner world, rather than cognitive thinking patterns.

In the eighth session, Mary was very distressed. She described several upsetting experiences involving herself and her family, and was feeling lost about what to do. After some time was spent listening to these concerns, the music therapist asked what Mary needed today. Mary wanted to focus on herself and take some time out from all the pressures. The music therapist reflected that it might not be a good day for diving deeply into unconscious material, since Mary was unsettled, and she may not be able to use the process for exploration and self-analysis. The music therapist therefore agreed that they use their time together for calming down and taking a break from the challenges in her week. Mary expressed relief and excitement at the opportunity to do what she needed.

The music therapist decided to focus on one piece of music that could be repeated if helpful. She wanted it to be reasonably long and stable, so that it would provide some containment for Mary's time to herself. She reflected on several options – beginning with the gentle, impressionistic style of Debussy's *Prelude to the Afternoon of a Faun*, but decided it might be too evocative. She then considered the predictable style and structure of the Baroque period, considering Pachelbel's *Canon*, but decided it might be too sad because of the descending melodic lines. Ultimately, she settled on the Estonian composition by Arvo Pärt, *Spiegel im Spiegel* ('Mirror(s) in the mirror'). Lasting nearly 10 minutes, this piece was beautiful, peaceful and consistent, and with only two instruments, it was spacious and meditative.

The music therapist then suggested that Mary might like to draw or write as the music played, keeping her eyes open so that she didn't go into a semi-conscious state. Mary had often used drawing in the past, and she would also frequently talk while she drew, describing what her drawing was about. On this day, she chose to write words that came to her mind while the music played. She did this without speaking, and then read the narrative to the music therapist afterwards. She described a young friend whose life was challenging and how many different points of pain and anguish this young woman had to endure. She described how that intersected with the lives of her own children, and how she could 'see' what she needed to do.

Even though the purpose of the music listening had been to distract from the difficulties in Mary's life, she ultimately did choose to process them gently and descriptively through the music listening and narrative experience. She felt calmer after doing this, and described having some distance from the experience, rather than feeling it was on top of her. As the session came to a close, she sighed deeply and asked about the next time they would meet.

CONTRAINDICATIONS

Contraindications for using focused listening with a client include having a limited ability to focus. For example, patients who have a brain injury or experience cognitive confusion may not be able to focus on listening for more than a few minutes, and may therefore not gain the benefit from listening.

Focused listening may also be contraindicated for people who are unable to relay their experiences verbally. In this scenario the therapist may be unaware of what type of experience the person has had, for example if the participant is feeling worse than before. Therefore, an ability to express the experience verbally, or through drawing, is often necessary.

A lack of insight into unhealthy rumination can also be a contraindication of focused listening. As discussed, unhealthy music listening can involve ruminating on a song that has a negative message, and after repeated hearings the person may feel worse, not better.

In the following chapter we articulate specific methods for using some of these concepts. The structure of playlists will be our focus.

Chapter 4

Playlist Construction

INTRODUCTION

'Playlist' is new terminology that has come into common parlance in response to our increased access to music through new technologies. In the time of record players, there was no easy way to create a 'playlist' because there was no independent recording technology – a playlist was created by the record producers or radio programmers, but not individually. However, with the advent of tape recorders, it became possible to take songs from different places and gather them together on a 'mixed tape'. This evolution in technological possibilities made it feasible to record songs from other tapes and even from the radio. This would sometimes require sitting with fingers perched on the 'play' and 'record' buttons and pressing them down, usually with a sense of urgency, once the DJ announced the song you wanted was coming up next. The mixed tape was truly miraculous in its time, and usually comprised a sequence of favourite songs, or a sequence of songs that someone else had lovingly made for you (a true gift!). However, technology continued to evolve to meet people's demands for sequencing their own playlists, and although this did create copyright issues and financial ramifications for musicians that have also multiplied in parallel, consumer desire was a powerful driver.

At the time of writing, playlist functionality is built into most music software, making it possible for anyone with internet access to design their own sequence of musical pieces. Although this possibility is available, it is not always used by everyday listeners who continue to be happy with random playing of popular or favourite tracks, or listening to tracks sequenced by others. Alternatively, some people might gather music together into groups, like folders, but not pay attention to the order of the songs or their coherence. The grouping may simply reflect songs that the listener wants easy access to. The way we use the term 'playlist' in receptive music therapy is more specific:

> A playlist is *an intentionally sequenced and purposefully selected set of songs that are meaningful to an individual or group in addressing a therapeutic goal.*

Key to this are the concepts of music selection and order, as well as focused listening (discussed in Chapter 3).

REFERENCES TO PLAYLISTS IN THE MUSIC THERAPY LITERATURE

Despite the relatively recent access to technologies that enable playlist construction, there has been a long history of music programming in the closely related field of Guided Imagery and Music (GIM). Since its inception, the process of guided music listening has been based on the creation of specific sequences of music, purposefully chosen to suggest states or possibilities to the listener. Helen Bonny's original programmes (see Grocke 2019) were carefully selected and based on her intimate knowledge of the orchestral repertoire that she played regularly, both as a violinist and orchestra leader. Many people credit the depth of her familiarity with classical music as critical to her ability to select repertoire and experiment with its order to find the best sequence for purpose – such as affective states (affect release), nurturing and emotional expression.

Within the music therapy literature, there has been increasing reference to playlist construction as a method, since technological advances have made this more commonplace. One area of application has been in identity work, with initial experiments with the method being conducted by Even Ruud (1997) in Norway and Dorit Amir (2012) in Israel. Both these academics used playlist construction as an exercise in the training of music therapists, asking students to compile a list of songs that they used to present themselves, both personally and musically. Although intersectional identity theory (Crenshaw 1991) was not directly referenced, this idea is congruent with the use of the method, where students were asked to expound on a range of aspects of their identity. Avi Gilboa addressed this more explicitly in his expansion of the method with Israeli university students, where it was used as a strategy for transcending cultural conflict between students of different racial backgrounds (Gilboa and Salman 2019; Gilboa, Yehuda and Amir 2009).

Beyond the university context, playlist construction has also been used with other young people in schools and mental health contexts. Like universities, this method was initially used for identity work in mental health institutions. In Carmen Cheong-Clinch's PhD (Cheong-Clinch and McFerran 2016), the music therapist began by examining the ways young people were using music in their everyday lives during the onset of mental illness, and then explored how to use this music as a part of the therapeutic process using playlists. Her work showed how young people's emotional connections with the music were primary, and this then became the focus of sharing in her version of the method. In parallel, Cherry Hense's research (Hense and McFerran 2017) demonstrated how young people's musical identities often underwent significant changes with the onset of mental illness, and this led to the development of a playlist construction method that actively explored these changes in uses of music (McFerran *et al.* 2018). Other references to playlists in adolescent mental health treatment have been more recently compiled in the *Handbook of Music, Adolescents, and Wellbeing* (McFerran, Derrington and Saarikallio 2019; see also Cheong-Clinch 2019; Geipel 2019), but the sparse reference to the method in the literature belies the likely reality that this method is commonly used in music therapy practice with youth, since their preferred music is such a prominent part of their everyday life.

Further developments have been documented in the use of playlist construction as a method at the other end of the age spectrum. The first reference seems to be in the early 1990s (Hanser 1990), although more specific reports have been published since 2015 as people around the globe are focusing on the urgent need for elder care. Some playlist methods have been described that focus on promoting physical exercise for people following cardiac arrest (Clark, Baker and Taylor 2016). In Clark *et al.*'s study (2016), the music therapist worked directly with each adult to identify meaningful songs and to develop a playlist they could use to motivate and accompany their daily exercise regime. Interestingly, the findings showed that people's associations with the songs were more important than the tempo and rhythmic qualities, despite being used to promote movement. In another study with practical focus, playlist construction was used as a way of assisting bathing (Ray and Fitzsimmons 2014). In this case, the music therapist provided a detailed description to other members of the medical team about how to identify relevant pieces of music and decide on the order of tracks, so that the method could be used more widely in the team.

It has become increasingly common for music therapists to describe working as consultants when it comes to playlist construction, particularly in medical contexts. In Denmark, music therapists have developed special software (MusicStar) and hardware to empower patients to choose music suited to their needs without being dependent on the presence of a music therapist (Lund, Bertelsen and Bonde 2016). They have conducted several studies to identify various playlists that can be offered throughout the day and night and that can therefore be used independently by patients. This obviously means that the music is less personalized than it would be if the playlist was constructed uniquely for the individual, but it still serves a therapeutic purpose.

Similarly, a couple of Australian music therapists (Short and Ahern 2009) developed a set of four genre-based relaxation playlists for use in a study in a busy emergency ward of an acute hospital. Once again, the purpose was to offer individual patients some autonomy in selecting music to help them manage the noise levels and distressing distractions in the environment, even though the playlists were not uniquely tailored to each patient's needs.

A similar use of playlists has also been noted in working with neonates, where the therapeutic purpose was once again to reduce the impact of noise events that were potentially compromising the babies' development because of the busy auditory field (Shoemark, Hanson-Abromeit and Stewart 2015). Although this way of developing playlists has sometimes been referred to as a consultancy role, others have labelled this 'ecological music therapy' (Bruscia 1998a, pp.229–238), or 'milieu music therapy' in Scandinavia, which has also been discussed with reference to methods other than playlist construction (Aasgaard 2001).

MUSIC MEDICINE OR MUSIC THERAPY?

This highlights an issue that has been the cause of great debate in the field of music therapy – should music therapists encourage other professionals to provide support using recorded music while they focus on active music therapy methods? It is true that other professionals have shown an interest in using playlists to support therapeutic outcomes, seen first in Norway through Kari Batt-Rawden's PhD research into participatory CD design (Batt-Rawden, DeNora and Ruud 2005) and then Marie Skänland's PhD investigation of using MP3 players for self-care in everyday life (2011). Both these researchers were supervised by a music therapist, Even Ruud (2002), whose interest in music as a technology of health has been long-standing. This illustrates a reliance on music therapy knowledge, but not on the presence of a music therapy professional.

Other researchers reference music therapy literature in their rationale, but do not appear to have direct involvement with a professional they can consult with. Examples can be found in dementia care, where one report describes how a nursing student developed personalized playlists to reduce evening agitation (Long 2016). Another reports on a Music and Memories programme developed by social workers, which uses personalized playlists (Wagner, Lee and Mason 2016).

Since it is more feasible for other professionals to use music therapy methods that rely solely on recorded music, it is easy to understand why some colleagues choose not to prioritize playlist construction as a way of providing care. However, our experience is that few professionals can dedicate the time required to make the method successful. This is perhaps why Long's (2016) paper reports on a project conducted by a nursing student, who is not yet employed to have other duties and who therefore has the time to dedicate to the project. Or why the Music and Memories programme has been developed as a 'for-profit' model, so that the social workers involved can find a way to fund the time it takes. The use of recorded music may appear to be more straightforward than using active methods like improvisation, but in truth, it is every bit as complex, and requires the same amount of thoughtfulness, knowledge and insight to be able to provide safe and effective support.

There have been some attempts to make this process more efficient by utilizing emerging technologies. The first documented attempt was again by Carmen Cheong-Clinch, who worked with an online youth support programme to integrate playlist construction into an interactive web format (see https://tuneinnotout.com/factsheets/music-listening-mental-health). The web page includes guidance about how to carefully select music for purpose, and sharing is suggested so that young people can get feedback. More recently, an app has been patented in the USA that prompts people to consider their choices of music in playlist construction based on music therapy principles, but is completely automated (Pinkerton and Duggan 2020). These inventors have included a comprehensive range of prompts to help people select music that is helpful to them in serving their purpose, although there is obviously no capacity to monitor adherence or effectiveness. It is not just social workers, nurses, psychologists, teachers, psychotherapists and youth workers who are interested in this technique, but also web engineers and other support organizations.

We suggest that music therapists are uniquely positioned to introduce the method effectively and understand how to tailor it to the unique needs of individuals and groups. After all, many of our colleagues can also play a guitar and sing songs, but we do not use that as a rationale for ceasing our use of these activities. The ways that music therapists use this method will be the focus of the remainder of the chapter.

IDENTIFYING A PURPOSE

The key to playlist creation in music therapy is identifying a purpose and tailoring a careful and considered approach to playlist construction so that it meets that purpose. As demonstrated in the literature, these aims can be diverse and are always specific to the needs of an individual or group in context at a moment in their life while supported by the music therapist. The following is a list of the most common purposes for creating playlists (see also Table 4.1):

- mood management
- emotion processing

- life review
- sleep promotion
- distraction
- relaxation
- agitation reduction
- identity work
- relationship strengthening
- orientation and focus
- activity support.

Even if working with the same person, each one of these purposes would require a different selection of music in a different order, although some favourite songs might find their way into several playlists.

To identify which purpose would be most helpful, the music therapist would usually undertake either a formal or informal assessment. This might be integrated into a general assessment of the person's needs, based on referral information and reports from other professionals and carers. In this case, the music therapist may introduce the purpose they have already identified to the person during this time, and it would likely be a variation on one of those listed above. The music therapist would need to explain how creating a playlist would help to achieve the purpose, and assure the individual that they will help them through the process, both technologically and personally.

However, if the session is spontaneous, or if there are no pre-identified needs to be addressed, the music therapist might have playlists in their mind as one possible method for working with a group or individual. Playlist construction might be chosen because they have talked about how much they love listening to music, or because the organization has created a music listening group but has not identified what specific purpose that would serve. Although it sounds unusual, many people have great faith and strong interest in music, so they intuit when music listening would be helpful without being able to explain exactly why. In those cases, the role of the music therapist is to identify a purpose that could be addressed by creating playlists before progressing too far.

This can be done in collaboration with the people involved, by asking them questions, such as:

- How do you usually use music to make yourself feel better?
- When do you turn to music for help?
- What things do you believe music is good for?
- How do you imagine music listening being useful to you?
- Are there any challenges you have that music might help with?

These are not questions that most people have considered. Their use of music is often intuitive and habitual, rather than considered and reflexive. Therefore, using prompt questions to help discover if they already 'know' what they need from receptive music therapy can be revealing in a useful, insight-oriented way.

IDENTIFYING THE TRACKS

Once the purpose has been established, the next step is to spend time considering what tracks are relevant. Again, open questions can be helpful in prompting individuals and groups to consider the song selection. These should be related to the purpose that the therapist has identified, and aim to help people reflect on what they already know. This should be the preferred strategy for identifying relevant music before the music therapist makes suggestions based on their knowledge of the musical options that might be suitable. Table 4.1 provides a range of prompts that may be helpful for this purpose.

Table 4.1 Identifying tracks for playlists

Purpose	Music selection prompts
Mood management	What songs do you listen to when you are in that mood? Do they match your mood, or are you trying to change your mood to something different?
Emotion processing	When you think about your pain/grief/anger/frustration, what songs speak to you? What songs seem to describe how you feel when you are angry/sad/stressed? Do you know any songs that reflect your feelings about this issue?
Life review	What songs do you think of from when you were in primary school/high school/university/started working/had children/retired? In looking back at your life, what are the major events that come to mind, and what songs do you associate with them? What songs have been the most important at different times during your life, and why?
Sleep promotion	What music makes you sleepy? What music do you listen to when you're trying to go to sleep? Does it work? Is there a particular style of music that you think would be helpful for sleeping?
Distraction	What are your favourite songs that make you feel good? What tracks do you have strong associations with, that always take you to a certain thought or time? What kind of music gets your attention?
Relaxation	Is there any music that you use when you are trying to relax? Why do you choose that music? Have you ever tried doing relaxation to music? Did it work? What songs bring you peace? Are there any tracks that help you release tension from your body? Have you ever done relaxation work that was accompanied by a particular type of music? What?
Agitation reduction	What music do you listen to when you're feeling agitated/worked up/stressed? How do you feel when you're listening to that music in that state? Is there any other music that you think might help reduce your tension?

cont.

Purpose	Music selection prompts
Identity work	What songs do you know of that say something about who you are? Are there any tracks that reflect some part of you? Are there any songs that describe how you feel about a certain situation/place/time? Are there any performers/composers you identify with, or that you have things in common with?
Relationship strengthening	What songs do you both/all like? Are there any songs that you both connect to a particular moment in your relationship? Have you been to concerts/performances together that were meaningful to you? Are there any songs that might send a message to the other person that you want them to hear?
Orientation and focus	What songs do you most enjoy listening to? Are there any tracks that really grab your attention when you hear them? What kind of music do you find most fascinating? Is there anything you listen to that always makes you stop and listen?
Activity support	What kind of music seems like a natural complement for doing this activity? Are there any songs that you think would be motivating for you to do this activity? Is there a particular speed or style of music that you think would work best for this activity?

If and when the individual or group is struggling to select music to use, the music therapist needs to be ready to provide expert suggestions based on their knowledge of repertoire. This will incorporate what is known about the person or the group as well as the music that they seem to like, and should also consider all the elements and properties of the music, as detailed in Chapter 2, and in particular Table 2.1.

The process of identifying the tracks should be a combination of listening, talking, reflecting, considering and contemplating. The way a music therapist works through this process is dynamic and caring and is not usually focused on efficiency and brevity. The opportunity to sit together and listen through the tracks is as important as the final playlist. This emphasis on process over product is critical to what music therapists offer to their clients, as opposed to teaching or fixating on the product of the playlist at the sacrifice of the therapeutic relationship.

CHOOSING THE ORDER

Sequencing the tracks is critical to playlist construction and part of what takes time to organize, even after relevant songs have been selected. This is because a core belief in music therapy is the iso-principle (Altschuler [1948] 2001), which suggests that a therapeutic journey with music will often begin by matching someone's current state and then progress towards change from that position.

Ira Altschuler described the iso-principle as being 'the principle of using music identical to the mood or mental tempo of the patient' (1944, p.793). While Altschuler used classical music in his initial experiments with this approach, many music therapists have also applied this idea to improvised music-making, and Tony Wigram (2004) has described how the 'seductive' transition can be used to step from one state to another by changing musical elements systematically.

In applying this principle with playlist construction, the key is to begin a playlist with a piece of music that represents what state the person is likely to be in when they begin their journey – to match their mood or their energy and/or their preferences in the first track. After that, the sequence is determined in a stepwise fashion, moving towards the desired outcome.

If the purpose is anxiety reduction, the first track would be relatable to the person feeling agitated, then the next track would be stepping to something slightly less agitated, and so on. At a certain point, the contour of the tracks would move towards something more peaceful and then more peaceful again. It may take as many as 10 songs if the person is likely to be very agitated to begin with, or it may be as few as four songs if the agitation is mild.

Similarly, if the focus is on emotion processing, the iso-principle serves as a powerful guide to decide where to begin. 'What song is most powerfully connected to that emotion?' And then, for the following song, 'What song would you need to hear next to help you process that emotion?' And then further, until the question might change to 'What song would help you move beyond that emotion?'

This is the iso-principle in action while constructing a playlist. It provides a guide that helps us understand where a music therapist should begin – not by denying what individuals and groups are feeling and trying to replace that with something more tolerable. In true therapeutic fashion, music therapists begin by meeting people where they are, and then help them to construct a pathway out of that feeling, closer to something they can live with.

Annie Heiderscheit and Amy Madson (2015) described how they developed an objective scoring system in order to apply the iso-principle in constructing a playlist with a client for mood management. For each piece of music suggested by the client, they scored it from 1 to 5, where 1 was 'Depressed' and 5 was 'Hopeful'. They applied this system twice – once with reference to the music and once to the message of the lyrics. They then averaged the score (that is, 2 = 'Quite depressed' music and 4 = 'Optimistic' lyrics was averaged to a score of 3). They used these scores as a guide for deciding the order of tracks in the client's playlist. It is interesting to note that the client described starting at different points in the playlist once it was created, and what was most significant to her was the sense of care she experienced from the music therapist and intern in the process. She also felt the playlist was helpful in managing her mood, and she reported using it successfully.

REVIEWING THE WHOLE PLAYLIST

Once the tracks have been identified and an order has been selected, it is important that time is taken to review all the songs that have been combined into the playlist. The music therapist might sit with the individual or group as they practise using the whole playlist and identify any tracks that do not work in context. They will also take the opportunity to question whether the songs that were chosen continue to feel right for the individual or group. Knowing that people's experiences of music are dynamic, the music therapist should not assume that the client's first instinct about a song will be accurate once applied. It might be that there are additional associations the person has not considered but that become apparent in re-listening. Or the musical elements and properties may prove to be unhelpful because of the sequence, or for other reasons that had not previously been considered.

The overall contour of the playlist will not be felt until it has been pieced together; until then, they are individual tracks. It is important that the music therapist has a strong sense of where each piece of music begins, what range it has, where it finishes, and how that connects to the next piece of music. Not only do we attend to the overall structure of the playlist, but as musicians we also recognize that there is a range of states within a single piece of music, and that where one piece begins may be different to where it ends. This is not only true of classical Western music, but of many types of music. It is difficult for music to stay still over several minutes, as you discover whenever you try to improvise music for a stable state, such as relaxation, and realize just how much effort is required to stay in one place repeatedly and yet move beyond pure repetition.

In GIM training, where the playlists have already been pre-constructed, therapists in training are required to become familiar with the affective contour of the individual pieces and overall programme. They also examine the intensity of the programme to deepen their understanding of the playlist so they can anticipate musical suggestions that may be coming up in the music and that might influence the direction of a client's imagery.

This same intensity of focus is required in the construction of playlists by music therapists. Each component is important, but so is the whole. And ultimately, it has been constructed for a purpose, so music therapists need to evaluate if that has been achieved. It is often the case that a new purpose emerges, or that the process was more important than the product. In either case, it is our professional responsibility to be able to understand and explain how and whether it has been helpful.

Musical life review

Constructing a playlist for undertaking a life review means that the client and therapist trace significant songs from the client's life that outline their life's journey. The review might begin with a song from early childhood, moving on to school days, adolescence, courtship, marriage, birth of children, difficulties in life, celebrations from life, to songs representing the point of life that the client is presently experiencing. Clare O'Callaghan (1984) first wrote about musical life review in working with people undergoing treatment for cancer, and described it as a way of affirming the uniqueness of one's life and the significant events that have occurred. Although O'Callaghan chose to sing the songs with the client, songs can be also be gathered on to a playlist so that the client can listen to the songs at any time on their own devices.

VIGNETTE: Making connections with music

The music therapist sits by the bedside of Xui Li, a patient in the hospice facility. Xui Li is aware that she will not recover from her illness, and is enthusiastic about the idea of compiling a playlist of songs that she can share with her family and leave with them as a legacy. The music therapist begins by asking Xui Li to reflect on songs that she recalls from her childhood. This immediately connects to the patient's relationship with her father, who was an erhu player (an erhu is a two-stringed bowed musical instrument). He would often play folk songs on the two-stringed instrument with his family, and it represented moments of rest between busy working days and weeks. Xui Li and the music therapist search songs online to find the most familiar ones, listening together and discussing the memories that arise as they do. By the end of the first session, they have selected the song that will be included, and agree to continue with the process in the next session.

In this instance, the playlist order will be chronological, and the purpose of musical life review is addressed through the process as much as the final compilation, which will serve more as a legacy for others during bereavement than it will be for Xui Li. The process will take some time and will require commitment from the music therapist to keep records and ensure that appropriate recordings are used and compiled in ways that are accessible in the future.

Relationship strengthening

Music therapists are often lucky enough to share beautiful musical experiences with their clients in receptive music therapy. However, there are times when it is more important that the client shares these intimate moments with family members or friends, or that it is part of a group process. In this case, the music therapist's role is to scaffold the experience, ensuring that all technological needs are addressed, and providing modelling and prompts for how the process works. The music therapist is sensitive to moments of pulling back and allowing conversations to unfold without additional commentary, while also being ready to step in to help guide the process. In individual sessions, it might even mean leaving the room during poignant moments to allow the client and their significant other to share a moment in private. In groups, however, the music therapist usually has a more prominent role to play, even as they facilitate the relationships between group members.

VIGNETTE: Strengthening bonds between adolescent group members

'So, what do you all have in common?', the music therapist asks the group members, who have been attending the programme for several weeks. The group members are quiet, unsure how to answer such a big question. 'Let's think about some ideas,' the music therapist offers. 'Give me some suggestions.' One of the group members says, 'trapped', and another agrees, saying, 'isolated'. There is murmuring about the group as people nod and seem to agree. 'Is there anyone here who doesn't connect with these feelings?', the music therapist asks, carefully checking in with each of the eight people present by making eye contact and intuiting if there is anyone who does not feel included. 'Alright, our next task is for each one of you to think of a song that talks about this topic, or that you listen to when you are feeling isolated or trapped. Why don't you take a moment to think about this – check your phones if that will help, or do some internet searching.'

After a couple of minutes, one group member calls out, 'I love this song. It makes me feel better when I'm stuck on the ward late at night.' The music therapist walks over to look at the song they are pointing to, which is Nina Simone's 'I wish I knew how it would feel to be free' (Taylor and Dallas 1967).

'Ahhh, that's powerful. Everyone, can I ask you to pause in your own thinking for a moment so we can listen to Mustafa's song?' The group agrees, and the music therapist connects Mustafa's phone to the Bluetooth speaker and asks him to press play when he's ready. The group is understandably moved by the track and discusses their responses to different aspects of the lyrics, the singer, the genre and their own associations. Once the conversation has finished, the music therapist checks about including it on the playlist, beginning with Mustafa, who nods. 'Okay, we'll decide about the order of songs once we have something from everyone, but we are on our way.'

The end of the group is close and so they wrap up for the week, with everyone agreeing to reflect on possibilities to share in the coming weeks. By the end of another four weeks, the list has been compiled and the group decides to begin with the slower and sadder songs and gradually increase the energy of the playlist, and in this case, it ends with R.E.M.'s 'Can't get there from here' (Perry *et al.* 1985).

In this example, the sequencing of songs is less focused on moving from one state to another, and more tied to the purpose of relationship building. Constructing the playlist has given the group the opportunity to understand their similarities and differences, strengthening their bonds to one another and serving as a record that they can share with one another. There is an aspect of identity work in this way, although the shared topic of 'being stuck' is the primary mechanism for relationship building.

Functional goals

Playlists are very useful for supporting more functional goals, and although we use pain management in this example, there are some similarities to and some important distinctions from agitation reduction or relaxation. In each case, the use of the iso-principle and careful, step-by-step sequencing may be useful. However, it is important to recognize the difference between reducing a state (for example, agitation) and increasing a state (for example, relaxation). The focus on reduction requires a gradual stepping away from those elements and properties that represent agitation.

In contrast, a relaxation playlist might be vastly different depending on what the initial state of a recipient is. Many studies of music for relaxation (see Chapter 6) do not use the iso-principle at all, and simply use practising and associations to programme a sequence of tracks that are reflective of a relaxed state. In this chapter we take a different focus, for use when a music therapist is constructing a relaxation playlist that is based on psychological associations with the music, rather than focusing on musical elements that convey a particular state. It might also be used to distract patients from a medical procedure, which suggests a different approach again. As always in music therapy, the way we use a method depends on the context and the emerging needs of the individual or group.

Part of the music therapist's role is therefore to discern the true purpose of the playlist, as distinct from how it might be labelled, or the words the person uses to describe their needs. Some people may say 'relaxation' when they mean 'distraction', or they might refer to 'reducing agitation' when they want to go to sleep. Our ability to listen and understand and assess what people need is critical here.

VIGNETTE: Using music to manage pain

The music therapist sits at the bedside of the patient, who has experienced significant burns and is subjected to painful procedures daily to heal. The music therapist has been referred to the patient to help manage these procedures, which occur frequently, and it is unlikely that they could be present with live music, so the focus is on helping the patient to develop self-management strategies using a playlist. As they talk, the music therapist clarifies the purpose with the patient. 'So, when do you think music might be most useful for you?'

The patient closes their eyes to contemplate the question. 'Actually, I don't think anything is going to help during the procedure. I can't imagine doing anything other than tolerating it. But after it's done, I feel so exhausted, and at the same time, hyper-vigilant. I just can't bring myself down. And that's when I feel really frustrated. I know that the pain is over for now and I just need to lay still and recover, but I'm so agitated, it's hard to lay there...'

The music therapist nods with understanding. 'How about we make a playlist for that time then? We're going to need to start with a song that is sympathetic to your agitation and frustration, and then we can move towards songs that will soothe you and give you a musical hug. But we can't just start with that. Do any songs go through your head in the time after the procedure?'

The patient contemplates the question before having a realization. 'You know, I'm so angry in that moment. It feels so unfair, and I know the medical team is just doing what they need to do, but it's awful. I'm furious. And I do have this song I love from when I was a teenager in the noughties, it's a heartbreak song, but it's fantastic – "Are you happy now?" by Michelle Branch [and Shanks 2003].'

They listen to the song together and notice how the verses speak to a contained rage that builds in the chorus with power and energy. 'Oh yeah, that would be a great beginning!', the patient says. 'Alright, then what would work after that?', the music therapist asks, and they begin to contemplate what track might start with high energy but actually has a more uplifting feel to it.

In this example, the insightful patient can articulate what they need and find songs that will work with prompts from the music therapist to help explain what will be effective. Other patients might need to rely on suggestions from the music therapist if they don't have a strong connection to music themselves but enjoy listening. In this case, the role of the music therapist is to make suggestions and encourage the client to listen to the tracks and notice how they react and whether it works. It is important that the music therapist is willing to contribute in this way, since knowledge of a range of repertoire is invaluable for those who don't find recalling songs easy. This might involve classical music, or it might be suggestions based on the client's identity markers, whether that is age, gender, cultural background, or other features. Obviously, it is critical not to stereotype people, but these more overt features can offer a starting point from which the therapist can sensitively proceed.

CONTRAINDICATIONS

Not everyone is well suited to constructing playlists with a music therapist. It requires cognitive capacity to reflect on different songs and consider how they might be able to achieve therapeutic goals. Some people may need scaffolding to be able to bring songs to mind, choose songs that are serving the intended purpose and even remember to use the playlist at the relevant moment. As noted by the references to pre-prepared playlists in some medical settings described in the introduction to this book, there are times when people do not have capacity to do the thinking and would benefit best from having a carefully selected playlist available during their time of need.

Similarly, a certain amount of cognitive capacity is necessary to be able to focus on the music. Many people are used to having music playing in the background, and as described in some of the other vignettes in this book, this can serve the purpose of reducing the impact of loud, unpredictable and frightening noises in busy hospital environments. When people are not aware enough to make these choices themselves, it once again becomes the music therapist's responsibility to select music that is within the appropriate parameters for auditory and stimulation purposes, and to provide the required equipment, manage volume levels, and so on. This is quite different to the illustrations shared that require the client to focus on the songs while they are playing for them to accrue benefits from it.

Similarly, some people may find music to be disturbing and suggestive of images or ideas that are difficult to self-contain. For example, people living with schizophrenia may find that music triggers paranoid thinking, and that hidden messages and suggestions may emerge when listening that are counterproductive. Other clients may not have realized that the songs they have chosen are associated with traumatic memories because they did not come into consciousness while the therapist was there, but which did when they were on their own. One role of the music therapist is therefore to follow up on people's experiences of using the playlist and to adjust and change based on the feedback received. Sometimes, they might discover that music is not appropriate for an individual at that time, even if it has been useful at other times in their life.

Part of the power of constructing playlists is the development of habits and patterns of physical responses that can become associated with the music. If people have successful experiences of using the music to manage their mood, to sleep or to share with others, they are more likely to do it again and with greater expectation of what will be achieved. This makes success increasingly likely, in what Tia DeNora (2021) describes as the 'placebo effect' of music. However, the opposite can also occur. Some people may find that they begin to associate the playlist with negative thinking patterns or behaviour, such as suicidal ideation or dangerous behaviours. Once again, the music therapist is responsible for following up and asking specifically about such possibilities, and then making recommendations about whether playlist listening should continue.

Finally, choosing songs in groups is always a complex process. The purpose of coming to agreements about what songs will be included in the playlist is to promote bonding and shared identification with an experience. The music therapist needs to be skilled in facilitating these discussions, since they will often give rise to complex interpersonal dynamics. Songs that have a particular meaning to one person may have quite the opposite meaning to another, for example. This needs to be negotiated carefully by the therapist between group members who might be passionate about their own musical meanings. In some cases, it may mean that particular songs cannot be included, and this can be difficult for group members to accept.

As always, the music therapist may need to grapple with their own associations with songs and genres. When working with people who choose songs that we, therapists, find misogynistic, or aggressive, or depressing, or distasteful, it can be difficult to tolerate the meanings they have for our clients. While there is some value in articulating our own reactions to music, this is not always the case, since our role is to be non-judgemental and to accept people's musical preferences. The decision to share difficult reactions to a client's music needs to be carefully and reflexively examined before deciding to proceed. It is not realistic to have a firm rule for these circumstances, but the guiding idea is to seek to understand the meanings our clients associate with different pieces of music, and not to project our own responses. However, there will be occasions when it feels appropriate to place limits on musical selections, such as not including songs with swearing in schools where swearing is not allowed.

CONCLUSION

Although playlists are a powerful method for use in receptive music therapy, there is limited literature describing this process because it is a relatively recent phenomenon that has come about due to new technologies.

There is some confusion in the literature about different types of playlists, particularly those that have been pre-selected as compared to those that are individually tailored for purpose based on client selection. However, all types of playlists have their place in the professional toolkit of a music therapist. Sometimes we need to make expert selections and other times we can guide this decision-making process based on the clients' preferences. However, it is our attention to musical parameters, meanings and associations, as well as the careful sequencing of tracks for purpose, that is critical to our professional endeavours. In this way, all kinds of playlists may be constructed within a receptive music therapy process, and this will respond to the unique needs and abilities of people in the moment of the encounter.

Chapter 5

Song Discussion and Lyric Analysis

INTRODUCTION

The first references to listening to and discussing songs as a music therapy method can be found in the literature of the 1960s when Becky Butler (1966) described the efficacy of music for stimulating discussion and introducing relevant topics in a non-threatening and encouraging way. Later, psychiatrist Lee Baumel (1973) contributed to the music therapy literature and described his impressions about songs as a forum for patients to 'tell the group more about himself [sic], to tell it in a less defensive way, to promote his own catharsis, to probe for identification hooks with other patients' (1973, p.84). Erdonmez [Grocke] (1977) then developed these ideas in her music therapy practice in inpatient mental health, also asking clients to contribute songs that were meaningful to them. From there, passing references appear in the 1980s by practitioners working with teenagers, with Marsha Wooten (1992) describing the value of communicating through lyrics and Darlene Brooks (1989) describing music as a bridge to reach the patient and as a means for introducing and discussing alternative coping skills. Deborah Salmon (1989) then expands the song discussion literature into her work in palliative care, where she found familiar songs to be a powerful medium for encouraging participation and evoking memories to be reflected on for meaning by the listener. She used the discussion time following the songs as an opportunity for self-expression, noting the delicate and gentle way that topics could be introduced and expanded on as appropriate.

Some of these professionals relied on expert-selected music, and as early as the first literature, therapists recognized that this could lead to the 'accidental' projection of the leader's issues onto the musical choices for the session (Butler 1966). This is a theme that has re-emerged in more recent literature, and Susan Gardstrom and James Hiller (2010) warn that the therapist may choose a song to meet their own emotional needs, or alternatively, avoid a song for personal reasons. Edith Lecourt (1998) looked at this another way, however, and suggested that music therapists may effectively utilize the process of complementary identification, drawing empathically on their perception of the client's experience to provide music that is relevant and helpful to the process of therapy.

However, it is mostly the client's projections onto songs that have been the focus of discussion. Cora Díaz de Chumaceiro (1992) described the concept of 'songs of transference', or what Sigmund Freud referred to as the 'haunting melody' in his introductory lectures on psychoanalysis. Although Freud was known to be dismissive of the arts and found them too confronting, one of Freud's students, Theodor Reik (1953), went on to discuss how songs on the mind could be used as part of therapy because they may reveal repressed ideas and feelings that the client was not conscious of.

Kenneth Bruscia (1998b) seems to agree, and rather poetically describes the role of songs in our lives in the following way:

> Songs are the ways that human beings explore emotions. They express who we are and how we feel, they bring us closer to others, they keep us company when we are alone. They articulate our beliefs and values. As the years pass, songs bear witness to our lives. They allow us to relive the past, to examine the present and to voice our dreams for the future. Songs weave the tales of our joys and sorrows, they reveal our innermost secrets, and they express our hopes and disappointments, our fears, and triumphs. They are our musical diaries. They are the sounds of our personal development. (Bruscia 1998b, p.10)

Bruscia also suggests that songs can provide an effective vehicle for emotional work, and, like Grocke, emphasizes the value of asking clients to contribute songs to communicate something about themselves (1998b, p.11). He believes that the act of shared listening affords a living through and re-experiencing of the issues and feelings presented in the song, and distinguishes this from a verbal analytic process that does not incorporate shared listening. In this way, it is musically active, certainly in the way that Christopher Small (1998) describes the act of 'musicking'.

Despite the many potentials afforded by sharing and discussing songs, there continues to be high levels of concern about the risks of working with recordings of preferred songs. Randi Rolvsjord (2010) has directly challenged European music therapists' refusal to incorporate clients' preferences into therapy work in mental health. She emphasizes the importance of preferred music and its function as a resource for many people in mental health recovery. Rolvsjord's position was established in opposition to many therapists who prefer to work with the untainted and improvised musical creations of clients, which they consider to be free of associations and providing a 'blank slate' for projections, rather than triggering associations. This fear has been shown to have some basis in experience, and Jennifer Bibb's research confirmed that singing songs with groups of inpatient mental health clients frequently triggered emotional responses that they then managed privately, without revealing their internal reactions to the group or the therapist (Bibb and McFerran 2018).

Our opinion is that this makes shared music listening a potent technique, and not one for the untrained. It requires a preparedness for unconscious reactions, transference, projections, group and therapist dynamics, as well as a sensitivity to the details of the music and the stories and meanings that emerge from the unconscious realm. It is not a technique to be taken lightly, but, as with all music therapy methods, it requires reflexivity and the ability to anticipate the most common reactions. This will be the focus of the remainder of the chapter.

CONSIDERATIONS FOR GENRE SELECTIONS

When focusing on song discussion and lyric analysis, it is both the words and the musical components that require contemplation. Many music therapists consider genre to be important since many people identify with styles of music – 'I'm a metal head' or 'I love country music!' being classic identifiers. There is also a large body of work in music sociology and musicology where scholars have investigated the cultural meanings of different music genres and the ways that they reflect the key issues of the time in that community.

An illustrative example is the extensive scholarship about hip-hop music, a genre of music that gained popularity in the USA in the 1980s and 1990s, created by African-American and Afro-Latino musicians in New York. Tricia Rose (1994), one of the first women theorists to examine this influential form, describes it as a 'highly rhythmic, rhymed storytelling' that represents underlying cultural politics. This idea has been further explored by a myriad of scholars (George 2005; Rose 2008), and, more recently, it has been considered in the context of wellbeing. Social worker Raphael Travis (2015) has outlined a process of hip-hop therapy, which seems a natural outcome based on Jeff Chang's (2007) assertion that it inherently embodies a resistance to oppression and the self-empowerment of communities.

Another illustrative example of the connection between musical genre and identity is K-pop. This genre of pop music developed a little later, but, like hip-hop, continues to maintain popularity and a strong connection to cultural politics. Initially known as 'Gayo', this South Korean genre of music combines aspects of traditional Korean music with other contemporary musical genres – particularly influences from the USA. John Lie (2015) describes how the genre both represents classic aspects of South Korean culture (economic innovation and cultural amnesia as examples) and blends musical styles into catchy melodies, point dance routines and perfect presentation. The link to government influence is frequently noted in discussion of the genre, both the cultural pride expressed by leaders, and a more critical sense that it is more of a global marketing success than a cultural representation (Shin 2009). In any case, the rise of K-pop that began in the 1990s is still strong into the 2020s, with songs such as Psy's 'Gangnam style' (Park and Yoo 2012) pointing to cultural markers, such as the lifestyle of residents of the wealthy, Beverley Hills-equivalent district of Seoul just south of the river. Less about resistance and more about pleasure, this transnational style of music is frequently considered to be one of the 'Top 5' most popular styles of the last three generations.

When selecting music for analysis via genre, it is important to be conscious of these large-scale associations that people might have with certain types of music, even if they are generalizations. Music exists in context and is not free of the broader social movements in which it occurs, and it may be extremely relevant to have some understanding of them. As music therapists become increasingly aware of their privileges, so, too, must they become conscious of what different types of music might mean to people from diverse backgrounds, particularly those with lesser capital in a particular country.

Beyond recognizing the contextual meanings music might hold for clients, music therapists have been trained to respect all types of music. Our background as musicians who can appreciate different styles and distinguish unique features of music is critical to this ability. People who have not trained in music are much less likely to hear some of the more intricate distinctions, both because it requires auditory discrimination skills based on practice and training, and because most people are only knowledgeable about those genres that are familiar, and often find new sounds off-putting or unpleasant. The degree of familiarity our clients have with genres of music also needs to be considered when making expert decisions about what music to choose. And as music therapists, this is inevitably bound up in the question of the purpose for which it will be used.

CONSIDERATIONS FOR LYRIC SELECTION

Beyond the musical features of different genres, lyric analysis also means that we must pay careful attention to any words that are associated with the song. Words could be in the title, the lyrics themselves, and even in the stories that are associated with the songs. For example, Kendrick Lamar's song 'Alright' (Duckworth, Williams and Spears 2015) has come to be associated with the #BlackLivesMatter movement in North America, just as Bob Dylan's song 'Blowin' in the wind' (1963) was associated with the American civil rights movement in the 1960s. Both songs address the issue of injustice, but perhaps also became popular with protestors because they caught the musical imagination of people of the time. Both provide easy-to-grasp key messages combined with poignant melody and rhythms. The specific lyrics connect into a far greater level of meaning, and so do many other songs in their associations to artists or films or other socially derived stories.

However, it is often the case that people make meanings of songs because they intersect more directly with a smaller story, related to their own life. As with both these examples, it might be a single line of the song that stands out to them, with other parts of the song having little meaning beyond knowing the words. It might be that the entire story tells a song that connects directly to their experience, for example Taylor Swift's long rant about her frustrations with her ex in 'We are never ever getting back together' (Swift and Martin 2012). Similarly, some songs, such as 'Time of your life' by Green Day (Armstrong, Dirnt and Cool 1997), have been influential over a number of generations; this particular song has become a graduation classic.

Some people who attend music therapy speak multiple languages, often because they were born in a country other than the one they are presently in. Clients often enquire tentatively about whether it is suitable to contribute songs that are not in the dominant language. Music therapists are also familiar with this situation from active song-sharing methods, and warmly welcome songs from different cultural backgrounds. In a diverse group, it may be important to anticipate this, in case members feel too shy to ask. It is sometimes an opportunity for quiet members of the group to speak more, as they will have the opportunity to translate key ideas from the song for other group members.

SEARCHING FOR RELEVANT SONGS

There are many songs and many meanings, each of which vary by individual, culture and need. While it has become almost impossible to maintain lists of such songs, as was provided in the first edition of this book, it is useful to be able to search online for songs with meanings that might be beyond your own known repertoire. It can never be assumed that the songs found through your search will be relevant to the individual or group of people you are working with, but searching will provide a vast list of possibilities from which you can discern what might be most relevant. We think it is one of the many satisfying and pleasurable professional tasks that form part of our role – searching for and listening to new music to share as part of preparation for therapy sessions.

To search, a simple strategy is to enter key terms including the word 'songs' or 'lyrics' and identifying markers of the client group, and then to spend time exploring the range of material that will come up. Searching may take you to online playlists, discussion forums for people who identify with the diagnosis or term, academic commentary and other people's perspectives.

For example, when entering the terms 'songs' and 'eating disorders', a range of lists and names of songs will be presented. Refining the hundreds of possibilities means skimming through the various web pages, which often include lyrics and links to video clips, and identifying those that seem most useful. In this case, two useful songs might be Marina Mena's 'Eyesore' (Mena and Solvang 2008) and Superchick's 'Courage' (Brock and Hsu 2005).

CONSIDERATIONS ABOUT WHO CHOOSES

As discussed in earlier chapters, the decision about who will select the music is key to receptive music therapy processes. There are good reasons for whether the individual, the therapist or the group is responsible for this decision, but the most important point is that the music therapist attends to this decision and is reflexive in considering the benefits and limitations of each.

Client-chosen song discussion

Client-chosen songs, either in individual therapy or in a group context, provide a context for the selection of the song as a 'projective' technique (Baumel 1973; Erdonmez [Grocke] 1977). This is frequently used in groups where the intention is that one group member chooses a song and presents it to the others for discussion. Several songs can be presented in this way within an hour-long group session, which allows for a range of voices to be heard.

Lee Baumel (1973) outlined a few ways in which a person may choose a song in a group context as a stimulus for the discussion of therapeutic issues. He includes references to selecting songs that say something about oneself, or alternatively, that are focused on other group members, either to reflect a feeling or because it seems meaningful.

In client-chosen song discussion the person may choose a song because the lyrics express something that they want to express and may not be able to, or they may choose a song because they identify with the singer, the singer's lifestyle, the singer's life challenges or the band. People are not always conscious of the reason for their choices, which means they may be surprised by how it feels to share the song, either with the therapist individually, or in a group. It is important for the therapist to anticipate emotional reactions such as anxiety, fear and embarrassment, and to be able to normalize and contain those reactions, while also working to dialogue about other meanings the song might hold.

The following points are relevant to both individual therapy and group therapy contexts.

PROMPTING CHOICES

When asking an individual to contribute a song, it is often helpful to suggest choosing something that is 'meaningful' to them. 'Meaningful' is a useful term because it is not specific, and yet it conveys a seriousness of intention. While it might also be useful to say things like 'a song you identify with', this is a complex request, and many people have not thought about the ways music represents parts of their identity, so they will probably choose a current favourite. Choosing a favourite song is qualitatively different – people might like the song for the groove, or because it's good to dance to, but it will not necessarily have any meaning for them. Similarly, asking for a song that is a favourite or is important can derail the possibility of getting to meaning, although it will undoubtedly lead to an interesting conversation. As a music therapist you will develop your own language for introducing this idea, but it is helpful to have a key term in your toolbox so that you don't stumble over the explanation or take too long trying to explain what you mean.

FOCUSED LISTENING

The song needs to be played loud enough to hear the words, but not so loud that it is distressing to others (in the case of group work). The therapist should make the comment that while the song is playing it might be helpful to listen and not talk. In a group, this can be done by first saying, 'Let's listen to the song now,' and waiting for silence before starting the music, thereby modelling a focused listening attitude.

MONITORING

During the playing of the song, tangible connections can be made, as the contributor or other group members reflect on the words and are moved by the music. The music therapist might make periodic observations of how the individual or the members of the group are relating to the song. The person who has chosen the song may show signs of feeling vulnerable, since they are disclosing something of themselves that could become apparent or be interpreted in a certain way by the therapist or by the group. The music therapist also scans the body language and facial expressions of the group members to get a sense of whether the song is meaningful to others. These observations will be helpful during discussion of the song.

MOVING INTO DISCUSSION OF THE SONG

When the song has finished, it can be helpful to offer a period of reflective silence before the music therapist asks the person to share what is meaningful about the song. The music therapist can stimulate discussion of the song by asking questions, and these can be graded to deepen the level of discussion; however, they should not be asked in a series, otherwise there will be an unnatural flow to the discussion. Balancing questions with supportive comments or reflections (as described in Chapter 1) will allow the discussion to flow freely.

Sometimes a client may want to talk immediately about the relevance of the song to their life, but for others there may be a feeling of vulnerability, so that easing into the more personal questions can occur via first- and second-level questions. It is important to remember that listening to songs is not a cerebral experience but often a very emotional and embodied one, and people may realize that the song says a lot about their current life situation, and may feel undefended in the discussion. It is essential to then 'read' the body language of the client to determine what level of questioning is appropriate to determine whether first-, second- or third-level questions are appropriate.

- First-level questions ask about the music:
  - What do you like about the music/song?
  - What do you think about the performer/band?

  These questions keep the discussion at a level relevant to the music. The music therapist can gain information about the client's preference for genre and performing artist, and can sense whether the client would like to explore the lyrics of the song.

- Second-level questions probe the meaning of the song to the client:
  - Are there particular lyrics that stand out as being meaningful to you? In what way?
  - Is the song meaningful to you in some other way (apart from the lyrics)? In what way?
  - Does the song remind you of anyone or anything special in your life?

  These questions focus on the meaning of the song, and can uncover information about the client from the lyrics, as these are likely to pertain to the client's current life situation. If the context of the therapy session encourages further exploration, the music therapist may ask about the relevance to the person's life.

- Third-level questions probe the connection of the meaning of the song with what is happening in the client's life at the moment:
  - Is there something about the song that relates to your life right now?
  - Why did you bring that song today?
  - How does the song make you feel?

- What images or thoughts came to you when you were listening to the song?

The music therapist listens carefully to the cues from the client to approach and engage in the discussion at the appropriate level and depth. If a client immediately wants to discuss the significance of the song to their life, then this is the level at which the music therapist should engage.

Barbara Wheeler (1983) has described a similar distinction between three levels of music therapy practice that reflect the purpose of the group and would influence the way that song discussion can be facilitated:

1. Activity-based therapy, where the focus may only be on the music, the band and the singer, and what clients like about the song.
2. Insight-oriented therapy, which may explore the meaning of the lyrics to the person and how the person feels about the song.
3. Re-constructive therapy, which might look at the significance to the person's life and the embodied experience of the music.

It is important to emphasize that these 'levels' are not rigid, and that people may function at different levels, even within a session. Much depends on the individual's needs in the moment, the nature of the client–therapist relationship, and the relationship of that member to other group members.

WIDENING THE DISCUSSION

If the song lyric discussion is within the group context, the questions may be opened to the group, for example:

- How do others in the group feel about this song?
- Are there other meanings about the song?
- Does anyone have something further to say about the song?

People can feel particularly vulnerable in the group situation where others in the group can comment about the song. If a group member is insensitive in their comments, or sarcastic or cynical, this can affect not only a client's attitude to the song they have chosen and its meaning for them, but also potentially their position within the group.

If the group is 'closed' (meaning that members of the group do not change over a period), then the group will be familiar with challenges by the music therapist or by the group members, and they will anticipate challenges to their choice of song. For other groups, where the membership changes frequently, the music therapist may need to actively direct the discussion if a client is in danger of being challenged. The music therapist can model appropriate responses by indicating the need for group members to be tolerant of others' beliefs, values and preferences. Statements such as 'It is important in this group that we respect each other's point of view' or 'It seems that the song has been meaningful to Muhammad, and therefore we need to show respect for his feelings' can be helpful. These statements can educate the group members about sensitivity, as well as help contain the group process.

At the end of the discussion, it is helpful to acknowledge the person who has presented the song:

> Thank you for bringing the song and sharing it with the group.
>
> I can see why this song is so important for you.
>
> Talking about this song has helped me to understand you better.
>
> It seems this song has meaning for several people in the group – thanks for bringing it.

Therapist-chosen song discussion in groups

Susan Gardstrom and James Hiller (2010) and Abbey Dvorak (2017) write about group song discussion scenarios where the therapist makes the song choice. In Gardstrom and Hiller's (2010) approach the song is chosen in advance by the therapist before the arrival of the clients and related to the 'therapeutic usefulness' (2010, p.147) of the song. They provide suggestions about processes that could be followed to facilitate song discussion while also pointing out that it would be 'absurd' (2010, p.148) to follow an identical process with every client or group.

Several attributes are taken into account, including:

- cognitive abilities of the client, their sexual identity, preference and familiarity
- key themes covered in the lyrics, and the importance of the therapist knowing what themes might emerge in discussion
- mood of the song, and whether the song is expressed from an individual or generic point of view
- qualities of the music
- stage of therapy for the client.

In discussing whether the song is presented live or in recorded format, Gardstrom and Hiller (2010) argue that many songs are too complicated to be performed by the therapist, and if the therapist is reading from a musical score, the client may perceive the rendition as performance. Another disadvantage of providing the song live is that clients may feel it is less engaging when it is not sung by their favourite singer, with whom they might identify. On the other hand, a benefit of playing the song live is that the therapist can control the speed and dynamics, adding accent to certain words, for example.

Dvorak (2017) proposes a framework for processing the lyrics of a song where the choice is made by the therapist. She uses a five-phase process based on a goal-directed model developed by Nathalie Kees and Edward Jacobs (1990) in their work in psychosocial mental health rehabilitation. This list moves from a foundational focus on processing the music, through stages of reflection and effect on group process, and then moving to personal insights and considerations for how this could apply in everyday life (Dvorak 2017, p.194). Dvorak (2017, p.195) comments that therapists may move up and down the levels as needed, demonstrating 'flexibility and openness to follow the lead of clients and of the group'.

A comparison of therapist-chosen versus client-chosen songs for song discussion

Table 5.1 sets out the differences between therapist- and client-chosen song discussion. Each has positive attributes, and each has disadvantages.

Table 5.1 Differences between therapist- and client-chosen song discussion

Therapist-chosen	Client-chosen
The therapist has control over the choice of song ahead of time	The client or client group has control over the choice; their 'voice' is heard
The choice of song may be based on current themes in the current therapy programme, thereby giving continuity	The songs can be on any topic; the choice is 'projective', where the client projects their emotions or issues on to the song, or the singer or group
Song lyrics can be duplicated in hard copy ahead of time, with lines numbered for easy reference	Song lyrics are described when the client responds to 'What lyrics stand out for you?' But group members may not know the lyrics
Discussion questions are prepared ahead of time, so the therapist directs the discussion	Questions arise spontaneously in the discussion; the therapist facilitates in the moment, without preparation
The therapist has control over the volume	The client may have control over the volume
The therapist may not know what songs will be chosen, and must draw on their expertise to manage the discussion of lyrics that they might be hearing for the first time	The client may choose a song that has inappropriate lyrics, or that is demeaning of a sector of the community, or overly aggressive
The client or client group looks to the therapist to guide the activity	The client or client group has ownership of the activity

RESPONDING TO AGGRESSIVE CLIENTS/ AGGRESSIVE LYRIC CONTENT

One of the most difficult therapeutic challenges is when someone becomes verbally aggressive while choosing and presenting a song, or when the lyrics of the song are offensive. Offensive lyrics can test the group members' values and it is easy to be unsettled, or even angry at the message portrayed, particularly if the lyrics advocate violence to another person, or demean another person. The therapist needs to carefully manage any reaction to the lyrics by listening to the client's explanation in a sincere attempt to understand their point of view.

Violent songs can be discussed in light of an expression of anger, and a typical intervention might be 'The lyrics of the song seem to be very angry, is this the way you feel?' This suggestion could be followed by a sincere hearing of the client's response, which may have nothing to do with anger, and therefore some repair will need to be done about the misunderstanding. This is the nature of the client–therapist relationship and should not be avoided. In fact, being able to reach understanding through discussion with a sensitive and respectful partner can be just as powerful as having been correctly understood in the first place.

If an aggressive/violent song has been presented in a group situation and other members of the group have become upset during the playing of the song, the therapist needs to address this in a more extended way. Once the client has spoken about their feelings about the song, the therapist can open the discussion to the group, saying, 'How do others in the group feel about the song?' This open question allows the opportunity for supportive comments, as well as non-supportive ones. The therapist will remain attentive to criticisms and use their skills to ensure that meaning is made from the different points of view of people in the group. Once again, it is natural that not all people in a group will agree with one another, so it is not necessary to avoid disagreement. However, it is important to bring maturity and wisdom to the conversation so that a resolution can be reached that allows for the different perspectives to be tolerated.

Sometimes the therapist must make a choice between allowing a client free expression of an aggressive song versus the capacity of the group to cope with that. It may be necessary to fade out a song that is clearly causing distress for group members. This might occur if, for example, the song advocates violence towards women and the women in the group become distressed. It is also worthwhile reflecting back to the client that the content of the song has impacted on others. This highlights that the group process is, in essence, a vehicle for interpersonal learning (Yalom 1970). If the group dynamics are particularly complex, it may even be useful for the therapist to choose the next song, to counteract the reaction to the aggressive/violent material.

RESPONDING TO DEPRESSED CLIENTS/ DEPRESSIVE SONG MATERIAL

A similar situation might occur if a client shares a song with the group that has depressive or suicidal themes. When the group is operating at the re-constructive level and group cohesion is high, there can be an open discussion of suicide within the group. However, if the group is operating at an activities-based level, it is probably inappropriate to have an in-depth discussion of suicide as the group may not have established a milieu of support and mutual respect.

The therapist may facilitate the processing of the song by asking the client what feelings the song raises, and then, taking the cues from the client's answer, either guide the discussion away from suicide (if the group is not able to support the person by discussing the issue in a meaningful way) or encourage further discussion (if the group has capacity).

Talking about suicide is highly charged and emotional, and a therapist should only engage in facilitating the discussion if they are experienced, or if there is a co-therapist to assist. Essentially any discussion of suicide needs to be contained, so that at the end of the discussion the therapist brings the group into the here and now, reminding the group members of the support they have, and how far they have come in therapy.

VIGNETTE: Songs to promote discussion

Six young people enter the room for one of their weekly group music therapy sessions. They are three weeks into a 20-week outpatient programme that they are expected to attend five days a week. Some education sessions are provided, but half their time is spent in therapy processes with their psychiatrists, occupational therapists, nurses, creative arts therapists, and more. Some of the young people also see the music therapist individually, where they work on individual issues using a range of active music therapy methods. Groups are mostly focused on receptive methods, including the use of songs played live by the music therapist, or using streamed recordings. The music therapist has selected the music for discussion in the previous two weeks.

The group energy is very low in this week. The young people seem to be dragging their feet as they enter the room and barely raise their eyes to greet the music therapist. After a simple introductory activity, the music therapist asks if anyone has a suggestion for a song to listen to together. The group is silent, and the music therapist considers sitting with the silence for some time, reflecting the resistance back to the group. However, after only a minute, she decides it might be more helpful to play a song, and has been practising Ed Sheeran's 'Save myself' (Wadge, Sheeran and Labrinth 2017) on the piano during the week with this group in mind. The chorus speaks to the coping strategies that some of the young people had been relying on – misusing alcohol and substances as a way of numbing the pain. 'How about I play a song you might relate to?' she asks, and begins to play the keyboard. As she plays the song, the music therapist watches the young people's reactions. At the end of the song, she considers what level of question to ask.

The group members have made some eye contact during the song, although the silence is heavy once the music ends. The music therapist decides to ask about the meaning of the song, rather than asking whether the young people like Ed Sheeran's music, or songs without a beat, or another question related to the style of the music. 'What do you think Ed Sheeran is talking about in those lyrics?' she asks, making eye contact with individual members of the group. 'Well, that's obvious,' replies one young person, 'it's about knocking yourself out to escape from how hard things are.' 'No, it's not,' says another one of the young people, 'it's about how people always treat you like crap, no matter how hard you try.' 'Yeah,' says another young person. 'They totally do.' 'Could it be both those things?' the music therapist asks.

For the next 10 minutes the group debates who is right, with people expressing passionate views. At certain moments, the music therapist punctuates the conversation with musical excerpts – playing a couple of lines that the young people are specifically referring to – before going on with the conversation. No one in the group expresses any identification with the situations being described, although it seems to be implied by the position they take. It is easy to assume that those members who believe it is about being treated badly by friends have had that experience, and vice versa.

The music therapist then contemplates whether the group members will benefit more from making their unconscious thoughts conscious, or whether feeling validated by having their experiences mirrored in a pop song will influence this decision. She wonders whether they might gain more from returning to the same piece of music and listening again, or playing another song on a similar theme to offer an opportunity to go deeper. There is also the option of asking the group members to explore the question of how Ed Sheeran's song relates to their own life right now, and doing more verbal processing, or perhaps drawing or creating a collage from magazine cut-outs that allows them to process creatively, rather than intellectually. On this occasion, the music therapist decides to move to another song. It is only week 3, and the group members are still learning about making meaning from the music. There will be time for more extended contemplation as the weeks pass, and for now, she chooses to focus on creating a sense of successful completion and energy. She asks the group again, 'Who wants to choose what piece of music we to listen to next?'

CONTRAINDICATIONS

Song discussion involves an ability to think about the effect of the music itself, and the meaning of the lyrics of the song and their effect on the listener. The person needs to be able to express how they feel, and to engage in some discussion of the relevance of the lyrics to their life. For this reason, people who do not have the cognitive ability to reflect in this way may not gain very much from song discussion. On the other hand, the ability for metacognition is sometimes the focus of therapy for those who do not demonstrate capacity to understand their own intentions, or those of others – often referred to as 'mentalization-based therapy'. This method could therefore be used as a way to increase this capacity.

People who have developed unhelpful patterns of music use should also be monitored carefully when introducing song discussion. Rumination is a common symptom of mental illness – a tendency to be consumed by constant and repetitive thoughts about something. Music can easily be paired with this pattern of thinking, since listening to the same songs on repeat can provide an excellent accompaniment to this unhelpful process. Therefore, clients may have developed negative associations with a song that are triggered through discussion, but which they might not reveal in individual therapy or group. For example, a client with an eating disorder may associate a particular artist with a negative self-comparison, triggering a wave of negative self-critique when the song is played. This would not be obvious to the therapist, and may not be raised by the client, but the music therapist is responsible for carefully questioning all choices to discover the myriad of meanings associated with a song and the feelings triggered by them. Since rumination is strongly associated with depression, this needs to be carefully considered each time the method is introduced.

Other associations with songs can also be difficult to predict, but certain conditions may suggest that associations between a song and their condition are more likely. For example, people who struggle with substance abuse frequently report accompanying substance use with music listening. Therefore, it is quite likely that songs put forward for discussion may remind the client of times when they have been using, and this might trigger a desire to use. Alternatively, since substance use is often a strategy for distracting from more difficult thoughts and feelings, a method that leads a client or group into difficult material might be too challenging for an individual, once again leading to a desire to use in order to escape the complexity.

The role of any therapist is to be alert to all the possible responses people might have when working through difficult material. Safety is always in the forefront of therapists' minds, particularly when people have had adverse life experiences. However, the purpose of therapy is to provide safe opportunities to process material in ways that have not been feasible with others. Therefore, it is not our role to over-protect our clients, but instead, to monitor carefully, attend to small changes in tone, body language and energy levels, and seek to understand what is happening for the client and to support them. Songs are powerful and they often trigger unexpected, or predictably strong, reactions. The music therapist needs to be conscious, caring and attentive, which will sometimes involve choosing a gentler approach – such as first-level questions – rather than leaping into depths that people may not be expecting.

CONCLUSION

Working with music that is meaningful to clients is at the core of many forms of music therapy practice. Song discussion and lyric analysis are both powerful methods and need to be carefully considered. This chapter outlines a number of key considerations, and many more will emerge in practice. As noted, some music therapists choose not to use preferred songs because of these complexities; however, our position is that therapy is a site for working with complex material. The music therapist should be able to hold and contain this complexity, and allow for meanings to be made within the safety of the therapeutic relationship. This receptive music therapy method is very powerful for that purpose.

Chapter 6

Music Listening and Music-Assisted Relaxation for Adult Clients

The purpose of this chapter is to describe the benefits of using relaxing music for reducing symptoms in hospitalized patients, and to outline the clinical skills required to facilitate music-assisted relaxation (MAR) for young people and adults across various settings and for different intentions. Relaxation for children will be discussed in Chapter 7, as we often combine imagery with relaxation inductions for children.

Throughout the literature different terms are used for the combination of listening to music and relaxation, such as 'music-assisted relaxation', 'relaxation with music', 'music relaxation' and 'music listening' (Howlin and Rooney 2020). However, in many of the studies there is no spoken relaxation induction as preparation; instead, they measure the effect of listening to music only.

Since 2010 there have been many studies on receptive music listening for pain, anxiety and stress relief. Some are conducted by music therapists; others are music medicine studies conducted in hospitals by medical personnel, or music psychology studies conducted with non-clinical groups.

INTENTION

The use of music to assist relaxation differs according to the intention:

- First, relaxing music may be introduced at the end of an otherwise active music therapy session, where the intention is to allow the person to rest after the activity. It is usually brief, and the intention is for the person to listen to music only.
- A second intention is to use MAR to reduce the symptoms of stress, anxiety or pain. The intention may also be psycho-educational, to demonstrate to the person how they might use music in their everyday life to manage their symptoms.
- A third intention is to use a relaxation induction (5–10 minutes) before commencing the music, thereby increasing the length of time the person is deeply relaxed.
- A fourth intention would be to use a relaxation induction as part of a more complex intervention such as a music and imagery session (involving the imagination), or a Bonny Method of Guided Imagery and Music (GIM) session (a psychotherapy form of music and imagery).

MUSIC LISTENING FOR SYMPTOM RELIEF

A large literature exists on the applications of MAR in managing symptoms of various conditions. The sheer number of studies has prompted numerous systematic reviews, many of them comparing music medicine (where the choice of music is made by medical personnel) and medical music therapy (where the music therapist is present during the playing of the music). There is agreement across these studies that the most effective music is that chosen by the patient/client. These studies and reviews provide evidence for the following conditions:

- pain reduction: Fidler and Miksza (2020); Lee (2016)
- stress and anxiety reduction: de Witte *et al.* (2020a, b)

- increased wellbeing: Giordano *et al.* (2020)
- lowered depression: Chan, Wong and Thalaya (2010)
- reduced agitation in patients with acquired brain injury: Aadal *et al.* (2021)
- cardiac illness: Bradt, Dileo and Potvin (2013); Burrai *et al.* (2020)
- sleep disorders: Jespersen and Vuust (2012); Jespersen, Madsen and Vuust (2020).

Relevant concepts

GATE CONTROL THEORY AND THE NEUROMATRIX

One of the early theoretical constructs in support of the use of music listening to reduce pain was Ronald Melzack and Patrick Wall's (1965) gate control theory, which suggested that an auditory stimulus such as music could block the transmission of pain impulses to the brain by activating different areas of the brain required for processing auditory information. Ronald Melzack and Joel Katz (2004) extended this theory by acknowledging that the experience of pain involves the whole body-self in a neuromatrix that involves interrelated areas of the brain that are activated in pain perception and pain behaviour.

In Claire Ghetti's (2012) review of 19 studies where music therapy was used as procedural support for pain associated with invasive medical procedures, she found that the gate control theory was the most mentioned theory in support of the intervention. Jin Lee (2016) also found that the gate control theory was mentioned in 20 of the studies he reviewed. In support of this theory, Ghetti states, 'Music therapy as procedural support may modify the various cognitive and emotional inputs to the neuromatrix by influencing attention, levels of anxiety, and meaning of the experience, as well as by impacting emotional responses through activation of the limbic system' (2012, p.30).

MINDFULNESS

Mindfulness is increasingly recognized as an effective approach to manage stress and anxiety. A central feature of mindfulness is to cultivate an attitude of letting go, or non-attachment, to accept what is in the moment, without judgement (Kabat-Zinn 2005). Listening to music may enhance a mindful awareness of a person's physical, emotional, aesthetic or spiritual life, particularly if the person can let go and surrender to the music (van Dort and Grocke 2014).

Mindfulness is not the same as relaxation, however, and in a study interviewing music therapists who adopt a mindfulness approach (Medcalf 2016, pp.55–56), one participant reflected that 'I took a little bit from relaxation ideas, but the purpose is not to be relaxed. So, there had to be something in the music that they could pay attention to and notice'. Another participant, a music therapist who works in palliative care, reflected that 'I try to use music that's not familiar. I also try to do that on purpose, so they don't have any attachment prior to the music.' The intention is 'to create a holding space that supports the development of mindful qualities, such as awareness, understanding and acceptance of the experience' (Medcalf 2016, pp.56–57).

Anja Tanhane (2020) has explored the connections between mindfulness and music therapy, as described in the music therapy literature, and questions whether mindfulness is necessarily the most accurate word to describe what has occurred during a music therapy session. Some features of both mindfulness and music therapy are similar. For example, she draws on Germer, Fulton and Siegel (2016) to explain that both have elements such as intentionality, being non-verbal, focusing on the present moment, and being non-judgemental and exploratory.

However, Tanhane emphasizes that it is more useful to recognize that there may be some mindfulness elements inherent in music therapy practice rather than trying to integrate one practice into the other, since there are also some sharp distinctions. She proposes that 'creative-expressive mindfulness' might be a useful term for music therapists to adopt when they are focusing on these overlaps.

COMBINING RELAXATION INDUCTIONS WITH RELAXING MUSIC

Several studies (Clark *et al.* 2016; Gallagher, Lagman and Rybicki 2018; Pasiali *et al.* 2020) demonstrate that providing a relaxation induction as a form of preparation can enhance the person's experience of relaxing music. Skill is required in providing the induction, as well as choosing the appropriate music selection for the client.

The setting for giving a relaxation session to a client will vary, from hospital bed, to an individual session where the client is in a comfortable chair or reclining on a couch. Ideally, it is a quiet environment that is conducive to listening to music, has dimmed lighting, and a comfortable bed, mat, carpeted floor or chair on which the client can recline. The room also needs to be warm, as the body loses temperature when relaxed. Also ensure that the session is uninterrupted. Place signs saying 'Please do not disturb' on the door, if necessary.

LIGHT AND DARK

In most contexts the ceiling lights need to be turned off completely, or at least dimmed. One of the most annoying distractions for relaxation is the flickering of fluorescent lights. Not only are they very bright; they can also pulse. Therefore, these lights should be turned off. However, many clients will feel unsettled by total darkness, so some filtered light needs to be present. Some lights can be dimmed effectively, or else side lamps can be used to light the room. The therapist, too, must have adequate light in order to manipulate the music equipment (if using recorded music). In some settings it might be appropriate to draw the curtains to darken the room to an appropriate level.

At the end of the relaxation session, it is important to prepare the client for a change in the brightness of the room. The therapist might say, 'I am going to turn the lights on again now and you may wish to shield your eyes.' Alternatively, the curtains can be opened again, slowly and softly, gradually letting in more light.

MUSIC EQUIPMENT

The therapist needs easy access to the music system. Although most people use sound from an iPod, iPad or computer, some facilities may still use CDs.

EYES OPEN OR CLOSED?

It is generally considered ideal for clients to close their eyes during a relaxation induction and to keep them closed while the music plays, as closed eyes block out the distractions of what is happening around the person. Closing their eyes also allows clients to access their inner state more readily. Some people are not comfortable closing their eyes, however, particularly if they are insecure about the surroundings, and need to have their eyes open to see what's going on. It may also be a trust issue for some, not trusting what might happen.

For clients who are reluctant to close their eyes, you can suggest that they avert their gaze, to look down, or look at the floor. It can be helpful to explain why this is necessary – to block out the distractions around them. Over time they may be more trustful of how the session works and be more willing to close their eyes. Note: sometimes people may open their eyes briefly to check around them, and then close them again.

VOICE QUALITY OF THE THERAPIST

The voice quality of the therapist is crucial to facilitating an effective relaxation induction or script.

- Voice tone and pitch: Your voice tone should be warm and calm, the volume soft (but loud enough to be heard); the pitch of the voice should be mid-range, with little dynamic change. It is important to keep the tone of voice fairly constant, so that the quality of the voice itself is effective in inducing trust in the therapist, and engenders a sense of safety – that is, that the therapist has quiet control, as conveyed in the tone of the voice. A high-pitched voice, for example, might convey a sense of insecurity or inexperience, and a very low voice might sound too gruff. A mid-range timbre therefore avoids those associations.

- Voice dynamics: In a normal conversation, our speaking tone has inflections that rise and fall to convey interest. For a relaxation induction, however, the speaking tone needs to be fairly flat dynamically, without dramatic rises and falls, so the tone engenders rest and calm.

- Pacing: During the relaxation induction you should monitor the pace by watching the person's breathing pattern. It is difficult to relax if a therapist is speaking too fast, as the person must process the words as quickly as they are said. A slower pace, with repetition in the instructions given, will enable the person to relax more easily. If the client is anxious, it can be helpful to start the induction more quickly to match the energy level, and then gradually slow the pace down, to match the intended relaxed state.

- Flow: An effective relaxation induction offers a phrase followed by a pause to allow the person to follow the instruction. There is a flow to your speaking without pausing in the wrong place – for example, 'become aware of...[pause]' leaves the listener in suspense, whereas 'become aware of your breathing...[pause]' allows the listener to turn their attention to the breathing pattern. Repetition of the same phrase allows the client to let go of processing every single word, and they are guided by the key word: feet, calves, knees, hips, and so on.

- Sequential order: To minimize cognitive processing, it makes sense to offer the key phrase in sequence either up or down the body. Asking someone to focus on their feet, then their arms, then their chest requires that they stay attentive to what you will say next, whereas a logical sequence requires far less attention.

- At the end of the relaxation experience: When bringing the person back to an alert state, your voice gets gradually louder. Note: for adults in hospital, the intention may be for them to fall asleep.

As with all music therapy methods, the basic principles need to be adjusted to suit the particular group and the facility where you work. In the following vignette, you will see how the music therapist adjusts different ideas to suit the mental health clients who are part of a therapeutic community that provides a range of therapy options. Here, establishing a distinctive environment that focuses on an aesthetic experience of relaxing is prioritized, using a candle and expert-selected music.

VIGNETTE: Group relaxation session for young people

The relaxation session for the group of young people (aged 18–25) in a residential mental health facility was always well attended and was scheduled for Friday afternoon, at the end of a busy therapy schedule throughout the week. They would arrive and drift around the room, finding the best place to settle down. The room had dimmed lighting and offered a range of cushions and yoga mats to lie on, comfortable chairs, and an option to sit with their back against a wall. The music for the group comprised Zen meditation music (Scott 1964) played on clarinet and shakuhachi (Japanese end-blown flute), and other music tracks including singing bowls, which provide a mesmerizing rich tone. In addition, a large candle was placed in the centre of the room, where a light gave off relaxing colours of blues and yellows as the flames flickered in the atmosphere. The instructions given to the group were to find a place that was comfortable, to be aware of the music, and to gaze from time to time at the candle, noticing the playing of the colours.

The benefit of this induction was that there were no instructions for breathing, noticing tension, awareness of muscles in the body or other targeted instructions. Because the instructions were open-ended they could enter into relaxation without any restriction or resistance. They also had the option of positioning their body in whatever position felt comfortable, rather than being given specific instructions. At the end of the session, the music was phased out, and the therapist forewarned them about how many minutes were left for the session, before gradually opening the curtains and allowing the natural light into the room. There was a brief discussion for the group about the experience, and the session closed.

CHOICE OF RELAXATION INDUCTIONS

There is a wide variety of relaxation scripts or inductions, ranging from short inductions and the count-down technique, to more extended inductions, including Progressive Muscle Relaxation (PMR; see Jacobson 1938), autogenic, autogenic with colour, mindfulness-informed, radiating light, and others developed by the practitioner (see Appendix A).

Several studies have compared different types of relaxation inductions. In Sheri Robb's (2000) study of state–trait anxiety in healthy adults, she incorporated music-assisted PMR, PMR alone, music listening, and silence as discrete groups. The participants were 60 university students. Although there was no significant difference between the four groups on the Spielberger State–Trait Anxiety Inventory (Spielberger 1983), music-assisted PMR elicited the greatest level of change.

Cori Pelletier (2004) completed a meta-analysis of 22 studies where music was used to decrease arousal due to stress. Six techniques were used across these studies: (1) passive listening (with instructions to just listen); (2) Guided Imagery and Music (GIM); (3) vibrotactile stimulation via a couch that transmits sound in high-density vibration; (4) Progressive Muscle Relaxation (PMR); (5) autogenic training; and (6) combinations of breathing, PMR, autogenic and/or imagery. A large effect size ($d = +0.6711$) was found for music combined with relaxation techniques in reducing arousal. There were differences, however, between the effectiveness of certain relaxation inductions, where verbal suggestion (autogenic) with music had the greatest effect on level of stress.

Varvara Pasiali *et al.* (2020) describe MAR for people living with an eating disorder. They confirm that MAR can reduce anxiety and stress, although caution is needed if mentioning body parts, as people living with an eating disorder have a complicated relationship with their body. While some authors recommend giving a relaxation induction that is a generalized script, Dean Quick (Pasiali *et al.* 2020) successfully used a PMR induction that he says worked well because of its step-by-step direction that decreased the opportunity for negative thoughts and beliefs.

STARTING WITH THE BREATH

Commonly used relaxation inductions begin with awareness of the breath and a suggestion for the person to become aware of their breathing pattern. Most of the time our breathing is shallow, using only the top part of the lungs/chest. Deeper breathing expands the diaphragm to the point that the chest and stomach open out. The breath may be constricted when the person is experiencing pain, and therefore maintaining a regulated breathing pattern that encourages the releasing of held breath may assist in managing pain and anxiety.

The typical wording for a breath induction is:

> ...become aware of your breathing...simply notice that you are breathing... the intake of breath and the release of breath...notice how your chest and stomach inflate as you breathe in and deflate as you breathe out. Notice the cycle of taking in and letting go...notice the breath is cool as you breathe in, but warm as you breathe out.

When directing a person's attention to their breathing, you can audibly model the breathing, for example, 'Breathing in...[audibly take in a breath]...and breathing out...[audibly let the breath out].' This can be helpful if the person is feeling self-conscious.

There are contraindications for focusing so intently on the breath. These are:

- When the person has an asthma condition, where focusing on the breath can increase anxiety.
- Patients who have undergone surgery and who may feel uncomfortable with a focus on breathing deeply, particularly following cardiac surgery.
- Clients who are survivors of abuse, who initially may be uncomfortable focusing on the breath, as they may have held their breath in fear at the time of the abuse. As therapy progresses, being able to release their breath can be very healing and helpful in reducing anxiety (Körlin 2019).

In these instances, you need to be careful when choosing which induction to use. You might ask the person how they would feel about a breath induction before starting, or you might offer a choice of a breath induction, or one that focuses on the muscles of the body (PMR), or one where they are aware of different parts of their body (autogenic).

CHOICE OF MUSIC

The most effective music for relaxation is music that is liked by the client (Howlin and Rooney 2020; Jiang *et al.* 2013; Lee 2016; Tan *et al.* 2012).

Asking an adult client about the type of music they enjoy is important for the effectiveness of the intervention. In a situation where a client is unable to speak, or unable to indicate a choice, the music therapist chooses the music. Interestingly, in Cori Pelletier's (2004) meta-analysis, she found that music choice based on findings from research studies, that is, expert-chosen, was more effective than music chosen by the participants. She argued that the participant may select a preferred piece of music that turns out to be too stimulating, meaning that the participant is mostly unaware of the elements of music that best support relaxation.

Many studies indicate consistency in describing the most effective music for relaxation, with the music having the following characteristics:

- The tempo is steady and slow, in either duple or triple time, as long as it remains consistent.
- The rhythm likewise is consistent, with little change.
- The melodic line is predictable, with a rounded shape, and a small range of intervals (often in stepwise progression). Although it is played legato, some effective music features a legato melody line with pizzicato bass line. The length of the melodic phrases may match the intake and exhale of breath, and repetition is a key feature.
- The harmonic structure is typically tonal and consonant, with a predictable sequence of chords, or suspended harmonies that resolve.
- The instrumentation is likely to include strings and woodwinds and exclude brass and percussion.
- There are few dynamic changes, which are introduced gradually.
- A supportive bass line is needed to convey security (Grocke and Wigram 2007).

A list of potential selections of music for relaxation with adult clients is provided in Appendix B. This includes short selections (up to 10 minutes) and longer selections (more than 10 minutes), as well as various genres: classical, minimalist, non-classical and new age.

In his study of Predictable Factors in Sedative Music (PFSM), Jeff Hooper (2012) asked music therapists to identify music that they enjoyed listening to that made them feel calm and relaxed (sedative), and music that made them feel energetic and wanting to move or dance (stimulative). The identified music choice could be in any genre. The features of sedative music were similar to those listed above. Hooper (2012) points out that the same piece of music can, however, produce different responses in different people (between-person variation), and the same piece of music can be experienced differently by the same person at different times (within-person variation).

In response to Hooper's article, Märith Bergström-Isacsson reminds us that the 'lived experiences' of music and the 'person's own music history' (2012, p.73) are also inescapable factors to consider. This is particularly important if the person has a pre-existing association of the music to a person or event that may impact negatively on their ability to relax.

Robert Krout (2007, p.138) also lists the qualities of relaxing music as 'slow and stable tempo (pace or speed), low volume level and soft dynamics, consistent texture (combination of sounds and instruments), absence of percussive and accented rhythms, gentle timbre (sound or tone colour), legato (connected) melodies and simple harmonic or chord progressions'.

In a study comparing two age groups and two different styles of relaxing music (Lee-Harris *et al.* 2018), Meditative Binaural Music (MBM) was compared to classical music. MBM incorporates binaurally recorded sounds, binaural beats, a slow tempo and gradual changes. The younger age group (18–25) found MBM significantly more calming than listening to low-arousal classical music. The older age group (50–80) showed stronger differences, evaluating low-arousal classical music as most comforting, followed by MBM. These results indicate that MBM may effectively contribute to relaxation, but results depend on age.

In Jennifer Fiore's (2018) study of online receptive music therapy for stress and anxiety in 23 college students, she paid close attention to the characteristics mentioned in the literature in composing specific guitar music for the project. She found that melody (with a fluid melodic line and small intervals) was the most effective musical element rated by participants to regulate breath (61%), followed by tempo (at 72–68 bpm) (48%).

Music with a slow tempo of 60–90 bpm has been shown to reduce heart rate and stress-related symptoms (de Witte *et al.* 2020a).

USING LIVE MUSIC

Melissa Smith (2008) provides helpful information about the use of live music for relaxation in her study that investigated relaxing music in the workplace of a call centre, an environment considered to be high stress. Smith selected PMR as the relaxation script and live guitar music as the music intervention for the experimental group (n = 40). The control condition was a discussion about stress in the workplace. Results indicated a significant reduction in stress (measured by Spielberger's State–Trait Anxiety Inventory, STAI) for the experimental group when compared to the control condition. She provided the PMR script simultaneously with improvised guitar music, commenting that she spent considerable time matching the quality of the improvised music to the script. Voice tone was also important, through vocally facilitating the building and releasing of muscular tension with matched voice tone. The improvised guitar music comprised broken chords, suspended notes and both major and minor chords.

GROUP SESSIONS

Conducting relaxation sessions for a group of people provides additional benefits in that there is social connectedness between the group members. Individuals feel less alone when experiencing music in a group.

The setting requires a room large enough for people to lie down or sit in comfortable chairs, or even sit with their back against a wall. If lying down, ideally the room would be carpeted for comfort. Other aspects to consider when working with groups include:

- The voice tone has to be loud enough for the person furthest away to hear you, which may mean that those close to you will hear your voice more loudly.

- It can be difficult to gauge the pacing of the relaxation induction, as you need to scan all the people in the group and assess what the best pace will be.
- It is difficult to address individual differences within the group, for example, someone who is fidgeting and struggling to be still. Depending on how well you know the group member you might move quietly towards that person to give additional attention and support.
- Choosing the relaxation script is challenging. If you ask the group what they would prefer, you are likely to get different responses, and so inevitably the choice of style is yours.

The following description provides a narrative of the principles and ideas offered throughout this chapter. It is based on our experiences of working with people who are seeking opportunities for personal development and growth, and for whom there are no particular conditions that are determined by the organization or their therapeutic needs.

> After welcoming everyone to the session, you can remind the group of the ground rules: if at any time a person feels uncomfortable, they might sit up or move from the floor to a chair, as long as they do not walk over another person's body, particularly close to their head.
>
> Remind participants to completely turn off their iPhones. Even on silent the pulsed 'ring' can be very annoying, particularly for the person who owns the phone as they imagine who might be calling.
>
> Allow the group plenty of time to find a relaxing place in the room and provide a range of materials: cushions, yoga mats and throws (lightweight covers) for warmth. Eye shades/masks might also be available for those who appreciate the darkness they provide. Once the group is settled you can ask general questions about the energy of the group members, or how they are feeling. Based on their responses you might then offer two, or three (maximum) choices of inductions. PMR is good if there is energy in the group, autogenic, or autogenic with colour (see Appendix A) if the group is in more of a reflective mood. Having given them the opportunity to contribute to the choice of induction, it is best to then choose the music yourself. For a group, the choice of music should be middle-of-the-road,

neither heavy classical music nor something like jazz, in case someone in the group dislikes those genres. If the group meets regularly you will get to know what genre is best for them.

Once everyone is settled, begin the relaxation script (see Appendix A), including the script for bringing the group out of the relaxed state at the end.

CONSIDERATIONS

Although no studies report contraindications for MAR, the following points should be taken into consideration when planning sessions for adult clients:

- Where possible, select music that is preferred and selected by the participants/s.
- Patients/residents who are confused may have difficulty relating to relaxation scripts that involve embodied experiences, for example, breathing a colour through various parts of the body, and may engage better with relaxation scripts that are short or have instructions to follow (for example, see 'Step-by-step structured/count-down relaxation induction' in Appendix A).
- Clients who feel vulnerable or feel they are being watched may have difficulty closing their eyes during relaxation experiences, or may need to open their eyes to make sure they are safe.
- Patients following cardiac surgery may feel discomfort unless correct positioning and support is in place. It may be appropriate with post-surgery cardiac patients to stress that they only breathe as deeply as is comfortable for them. Due to chest pain, a more upright position may be more comfortable in the first phase of post-heart surgery rehabilitation.
- Similarly, when using relaxation procedures with older adults who have physical disabilities, discomfort may occur unless correct positioning and support for the body (usually with pillows) is provided.

- Patients who need physiological support (such as oxygen or breathing support) may experience pain or restriction to deep breathing during relaxation, and the relaxation script should either avoid instructions about deep breathing, or include a comment, 'only breathe as much as is comfortable'.
- Residents in care homes for the elderly may feel uncomfortable or embarrassed when paying attention to various parts of their body in the presence of another person.

Relaxation inductions are also used as preparation for music and imagery sessions whereby music and the imagination are engaged to access creativity and problem-solving, and for the longer psychotherapeutic method of the Bonny Method of GIM. In the next chapter we address music and the powerful use of the imagination.

Chapter 7

Music, Imagery and Art Media

INTRODUCTION

In this chapter we address the combination of music with imagery and art media. The first thing we need to consider when discussing the use of imagery with music is the role of the imagination. Imagination plays an important role in our everyday lives. We draw on our imagination for creative thinking, problem-solving, rehearsing ideas and conversations in our minds, and in improvisation and song writing. The imagination forms part of a process of introspection, of looking within. Albert Einstein wrote, 'Imagination is more important than knowledge. For knowledge is limited, whereas imagination embraces the entire world, stimulating progress, giving birth to evolution' ([1931] 2009).

Sigmud Freud ([1924] 1956) also placed a strong emphasis on the imagination. His view of imagery was linked to his technique of free association where patients were encouraged to mention what first came to mind when a word/image was given. For example, the word 'red' might be anger for one person (emotional), an apple for another (object) or a stop sign (symbol) for someone else. Freud used this information to make his diagnoses. Carl Jung took that idea further in his technique of active imagination. He encouraged his patients to be creative in the way they viewed their dreams, looking more deeply at each of the scenes, figures or objects, and reflecting on what they might mean (Jung 1959). He believed that an understanding of the dream material came from amplification of the image (Chodorow 1997).

WHY COMBINE MUSIC AND IMAGERY?

One of the most reported difficulties that clients express when engaged in relaxation sessions is the presence of insistent and intrusive thoughts. These thoughts can change rapidly, such as scanning a list of activities that need to be done, for example, compiling a shopping list of items that need to be purchased to make a meal. Thoughts can be intrusive if they pass quickly, as the brain speeds up to process them, and this is counter-productive to being in a relaxed state. Similarly, a rapid flow of images (termed 'stream of consciousness') may interfere with a state of relaxation.

Including a simple visualization helps the brain become focused. As the therapist directs the client's attention to the visualization, and invites the client to look more deeply into it, the visual field literally narrows to focus. Focusing or centring is a necessary part of the relaxation process where the therapeutic intention is for the mind to be quiet and still. In addition, imagery and visualizations have been shown to help hospitalized patients in the management of pain and stress (see Chapter 6). Inviting a patient to recall a favourite place enables them to mentally move out of the confines of a hospital bed, to 'escape' for a period to a place that is pleasant and less stressful.

Finally, imagery enhances the aesthetic enjoyment of listening to beautiful music, and so it is important to our emotional health and wellbeing. Most clients will be able to imagine a warm, sunny day and the sun in the sky making the body feel warm. There is a logical flow of imaginal ideas, built on a common experience. Some patients may imagine the scene as if watching from afar, but for others, the experience is described as being in the image.

TYPES OF IMAGERY

Kenneth Bruscia (1998a, p.125) defines 'imaginal listening' as 'the use of music listening to evoke and support imaginal processes or inner experiences, while in a non-ordinary state of consciousness'. Imagery can be multi-faceted: we 'see' images in our mind's eye. The image is literally a facsimile of the colour, shape and form of what we are imagining. But imagery is not exclusively visual: other forms are auditory (in the mind's ear), tactile (in the mind's skin) or embodied (felt within the body's organs, for example, the chest opening out, chills up or down the spine) (Grocke 2014). You might visualize a red rose. As the image forms (visual), you notice the colour of the petals and how they might feel if you touched them (tactile). You might also notice the thorns on the stem, and momentarily imagine what would happen if you pricked your finger (tactile). You might even recall the scent of the rose (olfactory), and that might lead to a memory of seeing a rose like that in your grandfather's garden.

These are examples of 'intentional imagery', when a familiar object or scene is intentionally recalled. Intentional imagery can also allow us to try something out before committing to it – we imagine how something might turn out, as if to rehearse possible outcomes. We imagine the consequences of a behaviour as a means of testing out the feasibility of doing or saying something to someone and imagining what might happen.

Not all imagery is created intentionally, however, and music can act as a catalyst in evoking or generating involuntary or unbidden images that appear without warning. Music has great power in stimulating the imagination, as seen in film scores.

Music for stimulating the imagination

The choice of music for stimulating imagery may be based on the preferences of the individual or group. In the case of individual therapy, you can play a little sample of the music and check with the person if they like it. Ask them to close their eyes and notice if anything comes to mind. By offering to play through different options first, you give the person a choice and some control.

Selecting the music for these kinds of functions can be challenging, especially when working with groups, where it is not possible to find the 'right' piece of music for every person. Therefore, the therapist needs to make the choice.

The following elements are generally considered important for music to stimulate the imagination. These differ from those for relaxation, as listed in Chapter 6.

Music for stimulating the imagination:

- The tempo may fluctuate between slow and fast, or have unpredictable changes.
- The melodic line may include large, intervallic leaps.
- The harmonic structure may include dissonances and unexpected twists and turns.
- Instrumentation can include brass, strings or percussion (drums).
- The use of accents, staccato effects and syncopation can add to the energy.
- Dynamic changes occur throughout – a change in instrumentation can bring a new and exciting perspective.
- Repetition can be a key feature.
- There may be unpredictable changes in textures – thin texture followed by a full, textured sound.
- The bass line may be unpredictable or have a syncopated rhythm.

The elements that are different from relaxing music are tempo (faster), melodic line (more leaps to create interest), harmonic changes that can introduce unexpected change and therefore stimulate imagery, changing dynamics and accents, such as staccato and syncopation, and a wider range of instruments, including brass and percussion.

MUSIC IMAGERY FOR CHILDREN

Children have very active imaginations, and we use music and imagery with children either individually or in groups. Children may close their eyes briefly, but often open them again to see what's happening. They continue to be engaged in the imagery, even with their eyes open.

We can use music and imagery to help them relax, or to reduce anxiety about a procedure, or to divert attention away if they are in pain. For young children the script needs to be short and have a description that engages their imagination quickly. You can play live music or recorded music in the background while reading the script.

Favourite place imagery

The most common script is the 'favourite place' – this could be a place at home, or a hiding place somewhere. The script needs to give options for the child to choose where they want to be. A suggested wording is:

> Imagine you are in your favourite place...it might be outside...or inside... it might be a secret place...think about that place and how happy you are to be there...maybe there are other people with you...[add names if known]...or your pet [if the child has one]...feel how nice it is to be in your special place.

Breath induction

This induction is useful for children who are tense, anxious or in pain. We instinctively hold our breath when in pain, or we breathe in a shallow range, as if to hold the pain in. Focusing on the breath encourages the child to take in deep breaths, and the lungs expand, allowing more room for oxygen. Then, letting all the breath out releases tension from the muscles, and induces relaxation.

This is not a suitable induction for children who have asthma, however, as focusing on the breath may increase anxiety. Similarly, children may find it difficult to breathe deeply after recent surgery.

> Imagine that you have a lovely balloon...see what colour it is...now pretend that you are blowing air into a big balloon...you take in a breath and blow it into the balloon...take another breath and blow into the balloon... slowly it is filling up...bigger and bigger...and when it is a nice round shape, gently let the balloon go and watch it float up into the sky.

Cooling imagery (for a child who has a fever)

We can use our imagination to intentionally bring about change to a physiological state. For children who are hot with a fever, a cooling imagery script might be:

> Imagine you are in the mountains and the trees make this place nice and cool...there is a little stream with the water flowing gently...and a soft sandy place to stand... You can feel the cool water as it flows over your feet, making them feel nice and cool...and now you put your hands into the water...feel how nice and cool your hands are now.

Warming imagery (for a child who is cold)

For a child who is feeling cold, a warming imagery script might be:

> Imagine that you are down at the beach...imagine the soft sand under your feet as you walk along...the sun is shining, and you can feel the gentle warmth of the sun on your body...the sun isn't too hot, its just right, making you feel warm...

This could be extended to going into the warm water and feeling the warmth on the feet – and then on the hands.

Other imagery inductions for children can be found in Appendix C.

Music suggestions for children

Saint-Saëns: *The Carnival of the Animals*, 'Aquarium' and 'The swan'

Tchaikovsky: *The Nutcracker Suite*, 'Dance of the sugar plum fairies'

Cherie Ross: 'Music for dreaming' (www.musicfordreaming.com)

Music imagery for a child with mental health concerns

Children can also draw on music imagery in more direct ways to address mental health issues. Mary Reher (2015) describes her work as a music therapy specialist to schools in her area. She uses a combination of MI sessions and improvisation. She uses a short relaxation induction and then 2–4 minutes of music, and encourages the child to imagine scenes or stories. The child then draws a mandala (a free-drawn picture within a circle). In the next session she uses improvisation to re-visit the images with the child, and allows the story to unfold. In her sessions with Kate, a 10-year-old who was processing grief related to her father's chronic illness, the imagery was a metaphoric representation of what she was going through. In the first session the imagery was a 'spirit' – the spirit came out of Kate and created another little girl, who Kate said was a new person growing out of her. In the second session the imagery was of a magic fish – there was only one like it in the world. Kate felt that she was in control of the imagery journey with the fish. In the third session Kate imagined the girl, who liked to go to the beach, but one day all the water had disappeared, and she was devastated because she could not find it. Kate immediately saw the relevance of the water disappearing to what had happened on the fateful day her father had gone into a coma. In the fourth session Kate imagined a magic sun with magnificent colours. Later Kate grieved for the death of her cat in an image of a water slide (the water disappearing again). She said that losing the cat was like losing part of herself. In her final session Kate focused on the love in her family, depicted in the mandala with red hearts.

The parallel process of the image of the disappearing water was a conduit for Kate to address the finality of the death of the cat, and the impermanent state of coma her father was in. Interspersed with the music imagery sessions Mary and Kate improvised on the images and talked about the feelings that arose in the improvisations. This enabled the imagery to be transferred into everyday life.

Kim Archambault *et al.* (2019) describe a receptive music therapy programme for young people in a mental health unit. They use a method called 'MAP' ('Montage Audio Personnalisé en Musicothérapie Réceptive'), based on a psycho-musical relaxation. This involves the development of a music montage – selections of music that are meaningful to the young person which are played after the person is relaxed. Archambault *et al.* (2019) incorporate various energy states as well as relaxation, as there is a need for energy and vitality to enhance mood states when feeling depressed. In their study they provided four individual sessions lasting 45–75 minutes that took place in a room conducive to relaxation (shut blinds, dimmed lighting). In developing the strategy, the music therapist asked about the person's music history – music preferences and background information

– and a montage was created. The sessions offered a relaxation induction followed by the personalized music montage made from selections of music that were meaningful to the person. At the end of the montage there was discussion about how the young person experienced the music. Each montage was 15–20 minutes long and composed of four to seven 3–4-minute music pieces. The young person was then able to use the montage at any time during their stay in hospital. Results of the study indicated a reduction in anxiety and negative affect for the participants, particularly in girls, and in those 15 years and older.

MUSIC IMAGERY FOR ADULTS

You can create generalized scripts for adult clients in the same way as for children. Most adults will be able to imagine themselves by the sea or at the beach, or be able to imagine a bird in flight. Other common scripts are 'favourite place', 'being on a path' and 'being somewhere in nature'.

By the sea imagery script

> Bring to your mind a favourite place by the sea...take a moment to allow this image to come to your mind...it might be a place you know well, or one you are imagining for the first time...notice the colour of the sea... and the shape of the waves...notice the warm sand under your feet...feel the warm sun on your body...you might like to lie down on the warm sand listening to the gentle sound of the waves on the shore...notice how it feels in your body...[start the music]...and now allow the music to be with you and support your image.

Favourite place imagery script

> Bring to your mind a favourite place...take a moment to allow this image to come to your mind...it might be a place you know well...it could be outdoors in nature, or inside...if more than one image comes to your

mind, just choose one for the moment...notice what is around you...notice the colours and the shapes...notice where you are in this image...if you are alone or with others...and notice how it feels for you to be there right now [start the music]...and now allow the music to be there with you.

Imagery during chemotherapy

Debra Burns *et al.* (2018) explain a typical supportive music imagery session for patients undergoing cancer treatment. They describe the 45-minute session, where patients move through four stages:

1. Opening dialogue with the music therapist, to develop an understanding of the patient's current emotional state and goals for the session (5 minutes).
2. Transition to a more comfortable position (usually reclined), with the support of pillows and blankets for warmth.
3. Music and imagery intervention, accompanied by recorded music in which the music therapist guides the patient through a pre-agreed image, such as relaxing the body, changing the breathing rhythm and depth, visualization, and connecting with the patient's spiritual or religious world. The imagery could be a place in nature, nurturing images, images related to the effect of the chemotherapy on the person's body or positive imagery related to the person's life. The music is typically in the 'new age' tradition (for example, Daniel Kobialka), and is played free field (35 minutes).
4. Brief review, reflecting on the experience, connecting the patient to session elements of importance, and bringing the experience to a close (3–5 minutes).

Longer scripts

A logical step is to create longer scripts that incorporate a 'journey' of some kind. The therapist provides a relaxation induction, and at the end of the induction they read the guided script. The music may be played in the background while the therapist reads the script, or the music can be started at the end of the script. Examples are:

> You are walking through a field of grass...it is a pleasant day, and the grass feels soft under your feet...you see a house ahead of you...notice what the house looks like...as you get close to the house you see a path leading to the front door...as you get closer you walk along the path up to the door...notice what the door looks like...you open the door...inside there is a special person waiting for you...be glad to see them...

> You are sitting on the beach in the late afternoon...the sun is setting...the birds fly across the sky...it is becoming quieter...the sun sets over the water... it makes beautiful reflections in the water...you start to walk along the water's edge...you watch the colours in the sky...and reflected in the water.

Creating individualized scripts

A powerful imagery experience is created when the client writes an individualized script with the therapist. For example, for a hospitalized patient who is missing their garden at home, the therapist may ask about the garden – what does it look like? What flowers are growing in the garden? What are the colours of the garden? What are the client's favourite flower perfumes? An imagery script can then be created from the information. The music therapist then provides a relaxation induction (see Chapter 6), and either reads the script while the music is playing, or starts the music at the end of the script. Using the example of a client's garden at home, an individualized script might be:

> Imagine that you are entering your garden at home...you are walking down the path...you come to the bed of roses that is your special place in the garden...notice the colours of the roses...move closer to the pink roses that are your favourite flower in the garden...bend down to smell the sweet perfume of the flower...now look deeply into the centre of the flower and see the patterns of the petals...imagine feeling the texture of the petals and how silky they are to touch. Look around you again and notice other flowers in your garden...take in the beauty of this place that you have created at home.

PALLIATIVE CARE

In Maria Gimeno's clinical work in palliative care, she has developed two processes: Music Imagery Relaxation and Music Imagery Journeys. She begins by asking the patient for details of a positive, relaxing experience. She then asks about the shapes and the colours, whether the person is alone or with others, and how the person feels in the image. The key words form the script for the relaxation or imagery component of the session. One example she provides is of a journey that a client took with a friend. The journey involved taking a hiking trip and finally arriving at the top of a mountain. Because Gimeno enquired about the intricate details of each aspect, the description is rich and imbued with meaning (Gimeno 2015).

Group music and imagery (GrpMI) for adults

GrpMI will often be held in a large room with carpeted floor, to enable sufficient space between group members when lying down. Alternatively, clients may be sitting in comfortable chairs in a large circle. Usually, the music is played immediately after the induction (see Appendix A for relaxation inductions). The duration of the music selection will vary according to the context of the session. The selection needs some dynamic changes to stimulate imagery, but be well contained at the end, that is, have a definite ending to the music, such as a definite concluding cadence. At the end of the music each member of the group draws a mandala or writes about their experience.

There are several steps involved in conducting a GrpMI session:

1. Assess the suitability of the clients in the group for the method. In the group context each member should be able to respect the others in the group and not disrupt the group process.

2. The set-up for the session: a quiet place, a sign on the door to prevent disruption, a comfortable floor with mats or comfortable chairs, a sound system that reproduces music well and is positioned so that all members of the group can hear equally well.

3. Start with a discussion with the group to determine a theme for the session. It is helpful if the group has a common goal that they may

be working towards, or perhaps a common goal that has brought them together. The therapist facilitates the discussion, and then summarizes the views of the group and suggests the focus or theme. This helps the group have a sense of where the imagery might start, and provides an anchor for the imagery experience.

4. Suggest the group members find a place in the room (or a chair) that is comfortable for them, and encourage them to take some time to get as comfortable as possible. Usually, the group members need a blanket to keep them warm during the session and a pillow for their head. Dim the lights in the room. When the group members are as comfortable as possible, the therapist begins the relaxation induction. They might begin by suggesting that each person turns their attention to how their body is feeling, and to 'let any other distractions be attended to by another person'. This statement helps if a member of the group is unsettled, or if there is noise outside the room. At the end of the induction the therapist focuses the group on the theme: 'and now bring your attention to...and as the music begins to play, allow the music into that image, allowing the image to change as the music suggests'. This latter point is important in the group context, because the therapist has chosen the music for the group, not for an individual, so the match may not always be a good one. Sometimes group members comment that they had an image in mind, but when the music started it didn't match the image, and so the imagery stopped. It is therefore important to say, 'allow the image to change as the music suggests' – which indicates to the clients in the group that they can change the image, since the music cannot be changed to suit each person's experience.

5. Monitor the group's experience. While the music is playing, the therapist carefully observes each person in the group, noting any changes in body posture, facial expression or other indication of each person's experience, for example, tears, or a client turning on their side and moving into a foetal position. During the post-music discussion, the therapist might check with the client about their feelings to ensure that each person in the group leaves the session in a safe frame of mind.

6. When the music has finished, the therapist says, 'The music has finished...allow any imagery to come to a close...allow the imagery to fade.' In the group context the therapist needs to project their voice so that it reaches to the person furthest away. The therapist also needs to remind the group of the physical place they are in, since some group members may be still in an altered state of awareness:

   > Become aware of the room we are in, your body on the floor [or chair]...become aware of the other people in the room...aware of the sounds within the room [or outside the room if there are noises that are audible]...gradually begin to wiggle your toes and fingers, move your legs and arms, and give the body a big stretch...and open your eyes...

   Sometimes group members do not 'return' at the same pace, and the therapist continues to project their voice, giving it an 'edge' so that people hear more acutely what is being said. If a client is still not alert, the therapist might approach close to the person and mention their name: 'Justine, becoming aware of your body now, begin to move your legs, Justine...'.

7. In GrpMI sessions, it is common for the clients to do a free drawing or a mandala in response to their experience. The therapist can facilitate the drawing by saying, 'You might like to draw something of your experience – it does not have to be a replica of your imagery, but rather capture the essence of what you have experienced. You might want to draw a shape, or you may be drawn to a colour that will start your drawing.' These instructions help a client who feels unconfident about drawing. The group draws in silence, and after a period the therapist may say, 'Let's have another two to three minutes on the drawings and then we can share together.' This provides enough warning for those who are taking a lot of time over their drawing to bring some closure to the drawing. If there are time restrictions for the group, the therapist might also say, 'If you haven't finished your drawing at this point we might start our sharing while you finish,' or 'You might like to finish the drawing at home, but for the moment let's share the experience you have

had.' The therapist then facilitates the clients' discussion of their imagery experience via the drawings: 'Can you tell us something about your drawing – what stands out for you?'

LISA SUMMER'S CONTINUUM MODEL OF GROUP MUSIC AND IMAGERY

Lisa Summer developed her Continuum Model (see Chapter 3) for both individual and group sessions (2019). Using the same descriptors for the three levels of music imagery, she explains how the process is used within a group context.

Supportive music imagery:

> fosters the growth of trust and unity among group members. In the beginning phase of group therapy, clients need to develop a feeling of trust for the leader as well as for each other, in order to become fully engaged in the therapeutic process. As interaction increases and trust deepens, participants will perceive each other as not only individuals; but also as members of a collective unity. (Summer 2019, p.260)

The induction for the group experience 'should present a positive internal experience...that allows for increased feelings of safety, positive self-esteem and a strong feeling of being part of the group' (Summer 2019, p.261). The music choice for supportive music imagery includes 'either classical or non-classical music of five to 10 minutes duration with minimal musical development and considerable repetition to help the client focus on one image' (2019, p.262).

Re-educative group music and imagery therapy 'fosters change through insight. The re-educative level of treatment is utilized in the second phase of group therapy – the working phase – and only after group trust and unity have been established by prior successful sessions of supportive group music and imagery' (Summer 2019, p.262). The goals of re-educative GrpMI techniques are 'to help each client to experience himself [sic] in relation to other group members and to bring greater self-awareness and self-understanding' (2019, p.262). The induction in re-educative music imagery serves as 'an initial frame for the music experience and can be designed to stimulate significant differences amongst group members imagery experiences... Topics for a re-educative induction include the clients' current mood, a specific relationship, a current life question or conflictual life situation' (2019, p.263). The music for re-educative music imagery should be 'repetitiousness with little musical development but of greater length and complexity' (2019, p.263).

The re-constructive level of GrpMI therapy:

> fosters reconstructive ego change through personal and transpersonal transformation... Inductions are similar to those used in the re-educative level in that they serve to stimulate significant differences among group members' imagery experiences. However, at the reconstructive level they include an extended relaxation procedure to allow for a deeper state of consciousness and focus upon existential or spiritual issues. (Summer 2019, p.263).

Music selections include 'more evocative classical selections of approximately 10 minutes duration with a wide range of elements and more complexity' (Summer 2019, p.264).

A list of suggested music can be found in Appendix B.

Choosing the music to accompany imagery journeys

The effectiveness of music imagery journeys lies in how well you match the contour of the imagery with the music. This requires preparatory work on your part, to listen carefully to the whole music selection, and to make sure that the beginning and ending of the piece fits the purpose. The music selection ideally should have a contour that follows the imagery script. For example, a walk along a path aware of the surrounding nature, culminating at a lake, requires a music contour that is fairly flat but that has interesting sounds that might mimic bird calls or interesting sounds. Respighi's music has these features, for example 'The nightingale' or 'The dove' from *The Birds* suite.

Music to accompany walking to the top of a mountain to observe a view requires a contour that suggests ascending and culminates in a widening of sound to mimic the vista from the top of the mountain. The theme music from *Out of Africa* has those sweeping melodic lines suggesting wide vistas.

Similarly, music to accompany a memory of seeing a magnificent sunrise requires a contour that is undulating and gentle, but then begins to unfold and finally reaches some climax to match the magnificent colours of a sunrise. A good illustration is Grieg's 'Morning', from the *Peer Gynt Suite*. It lasts for 4:10 minutes, and begins with pastoral sounds played between flutes, oboes and clarinets. The main melodic phrase is repeated across these instruments. At 1 minute there is a crescendo (the sunrise), and further development. At 2:15 there is a return to the first quiet theme, followed by woodwinds playing a gentle reprise of the opening melody.

Over time you can build your own library of selections that you have found suitable for certain imagery scripts based on the music contour and how it matches the unfolding of the script as it is read out.

COMBINING MUSIC AND ART MEDIA

Drawing to music

One of the most relaxing ways to combine music and art work is to simply draw to music. The format of the drawing can be free field, using a small section of the paper, or the entire page, and drawing with oil crayons or painting with watercolours. Drawing to music is a process for reflection and retrospection. It can be used when the client is very tired, and expresses the need for something that is not complicated. Drawing to music may also be appropriate when you have had a challenging conversation about an issue and the client needs some time to reflect on what has been said.

At the end of the drawing period, there is a process for describing what stands out in the drawing for the client. It could be a colour, or a shape, or a particular design. Sometimes the client might be surprised by what they have drawn. Sometimes there is a figure that emerges in the drawing as you and the client look at it. Or the client may have a realization about the number of people that they have included (or not included).

Drawing to music can be helpful for clients who are dealing with trauma in their lives, when imagery is not recommended because it may bring up images that re-traumatize them. It may also be useful for clients who have a brain injury, where imagery processes are too complicated.

Music, Drawing and Narrative (MDN)

Music, Drawing and Narrative (MDN) is a method devised by Joanna Booth, a New Zealand-trained BMGIM (Bonny Method of GIM) therapist. In MDN, three art media – music, drawing and narrative – are combined to create a vehicle for story making. Booth (2005–06) describes the full MDN session as being in 'sonata' form:

- In the *exposition*, themes are explored, the therapist assesses the client's mood state and energy level, and the music is chosen. A relaxation induction is provided centred on support and breathing. The themes are summarized, and a working focus given. The client is encouraged to be aware of all feelings.
- In *development*, the client draws to music in silence while the therapist takes notes of the shapes and colours used in sequence.
- In *recapitulation*, the same piece of music is played again, and the client writes a story of their drawing while the therapist remains silent. New material may arise in the recapitulation. When the music finishes and the client has concluded the writing, the narrative is read aloud to the therapist and a discussion follows.
- The *coda*. As the session nears the end, key aspects are highlighted. The therapist, with the client's permission, may take a photo of the drawing, as it provides a useful visual reference for the next session.

MDN works as an individual therapy process and can be used by therapists for their own self-care. It also works effectively in the group context. The role of the client is to listen to the music, to draw and to write a narrative, so the applications of MDN include contexts where the client can concentrate for approximately 60–90 minutes and can express themselves in the media of drawing and narrative.

THE MUSIC SELECTIONS

Booth (2005–06) explains that there are currently 25 MDN music programmes ranging in length from 10–30 minutes, enabling a therapy session to fit within the 50-minute hour (see Booth 2005–06, pp.72–73; Grocke 2019, pp.690–691).

Appropriate music for this technique is about the speed of andante, and has a good balance of chordal and contrapuntal textures, with long, evolving melodic lines, whether accompanied or interwoven, as 'this type of texture encourages both reverie and drawing, [with] inherent stability' (Booth 2005–06, p.59).

TREE OF LIFE METHODOLOGY

The Tree of Life methodology was developed by Ncazelo Ncube-Mlilo (Regional Psychosocial Support Initiative, REPSSI) and David Denborough (Dulwich Centre Foundation), and has now been used in many countries around the world. It is an approach used with children, young people and adults to encourage them to 'speak about their lives in a way that makes them stronger' (https://dulwichcentre.com.au/the-tree-of-life).

The approach involves people drawing their own Tree of Life in which they reflect on their 'roots' (where they come from), their sense of self, skills and knowledge (the trunk), their hopes and dreams (the branches), as well as the special people in their lives (flowers and fruits). The participants then join their trees into a 'Forest of Life' and, in groups, discuss some of the 'storms' that affect their lives and the ways that they respond to these storms, and protect themselves and each other.

The focus for drawing the tree evolves around the individual person or the group, but might include the following statements:

> Roots: Who were the influential people as you were growing up? People who nurtured you and your talents? How might you draw the roots of the tree? Music example: Borodin, *Symphony no. 1*, andante (6:12).
>
> Ground: How fertile was the ground when the roots were laid down? How might you draw the ground? Music example: Bach, *Brandenburg Concerto no. 6*, adagio ma non tanto (5:29).
>
> Trunk: The trunk of the tree represents your values – what you hold to be meaningful, and what is of value to you. As you reflect on these, how might the trunk of your tree look? Music example: Holst, *The Planets Suite*, 'Venus' (8:35).
>
> Branches: The branches are your hopes and dreams for the future. Some

may be large, some small – how will they be drawn on your Tree of Life? Music example: Berlioz, *Flight into Egypt*, 'Childhood of Christ' (5:18).

Leaves: The leaves are all the people in your life right now. As you think of them, and the colours of their different personalities, think of how they will be shown on the leaves of the tree. Music example: Respighi, *The Pines of Rome*, 'Gianicola' (6:39).

Fruits: The fruits of your labours. What gifts have you received from your friends, your life? Music example: Delius, *Koanga*, 'La Calinda' (4:03).

Flowers and seeds: These are handed on to others. What gifts can you pass on? Music example: Dvořák, *Czech Suite*, 'Romanze' (4:32)

In selecting the music to accompany the drawing, you need to be aware of the associated elements of the tree parts and music:

- Roots: music that might begin in a deep register, is slow, and has long elongated melodies.
- Ground: music that is grounded, such as slow music of the Baroque period.
- Trunk: music that grows with a sense of strength.
- Branches: elongated melodies that suggest branches growing out from the trunk.
- Leaves and fruits: music that has different tone qualities and timbres, to match the different personalities of friends.

This method can be very powerful in individual therapy and in groups. Thinking of key people in your life can bring up loss and grief as well as positive associations with people. Music adds an emotional stimulus as well, and clients can touch some tender places in their lives. For this reason, it is important to allow plenty of time for discussion. Each person in the group should be given ample time to reflect. If you find yourself short of time for one reason or another, it is best to divide the group into smaller groups of two or three, so each person is not rushed in their reflections.

CONTRAINDICATIONS

As we have described for many approaches in receptive music therapy, there are areas of practice where music and imagery would be contraindicated. High on the list would be people who have difficulty distinguishing between the imagined and the real. People who are living with severe mental illness, for example, may find it hard to imagine themselves walking up a path in a mountain, reaching the top and observing the view. Individual differences exist, but it would be helpful to trial a short imagery journey first, to see if the person finds it helpful to their own health and wellbeing.

Along similar lines, music and imagery may not be helpful for people who can't see the point in imaging a special place. Some people can be quite concrete in their view of the world and may not see any purpose in imagining anything. A relaxation induction that is quite structured might be helpful instead.

Many clients may have a reaction to the idea of drawing to music, and may say, 'I'm no good at art'. We can be encouraging, pointing out that it can be relaxing, that they don't have to produce a masterpiece, but there might still be strong resistance. In that case we respect the person's wishes and offer something different.

Similarly with MDN, where drawing is a key component of the method, if there is resistance to drawing, then listening to music, or imaging to music, or a relaxation session, might be more suitable.

CONCLUSION

The combination of music, imagery and drawing can be powerful for many people. It embraces imagination, creativity and self-exploration, as well as providing opportunities for peaceful and relaxing experiences. A range of practical strategies has been described in this chapter that will be useful for those beginning to work in this way.

Chapter 8

Final Principles and Considerations for Music Therapists and Others

Other professionals could use many of the receptive music therapy methods if they had the time to study how to use music effectively to meet people's specific needs. They would also want to know how to predict reactions of different individuals based on a thorough understanding of that person and their relationship to music. However, most professionals do not have time to incorporate another professional role into their own existing job, so they ask music therapists for support in how to use music. This is not as easy as it might seem, since we understand how complex the musical pathways can be for each unique individual. It can be difficult to make recommendations without meeting the people involved. In this chapter, we gather together a series of considerations for ourselves and for others to keep in mind when these moments arise, based on our previous descriptions of receptive music therapy and other similar documents that exist in the profession and in the literature.

In this chapter we will provide a synthesis of the considerations raised in previous chapters, and elaborate on how they can be adapted for different people in diverse contexts. We will highlight what *not to do* in each category, since many of our colleagues who ask us for guidelines about using music listening are exceedingly positive about using music, and can be just as surprised when music arouses unexpected emotions and behaviours.

'WHY', NOT 'WHAT'

It is important to recognize that most other professionals will want to know 'what' to do and 'what' music to use. Our role is to explain that the 'what' is the result of considering answers to a series of 'why' questions. This is usually not apparent to colleagues, who will assume the use of music is simpler and more straightforward than we know it to be. It is therefore useful to be able to offer some details about the myriad other things that need to be considered. The following is our list of the fundamental principles:

- ☐ Know your purpose.
- ☐ People's preferences are *very* important.
- ☐ Make ongoing adjustments.
- ☐ Consider when to use repetition.
- ☐ Be aware of sensitivity to loudness.
- ☐ Decide about live versus recorded performances.

The list could be used to create a checklist of key principles for other professionals to consider when introducing music into their practice. By working through each of these considerations, they could identify any areas of concern for specific individuals or groups. Alternatively, it may be more helpful to phrase the fundamental principles as questions:

What is the purpose of using music for this person/group?

. . . .

. . . .

. . . .

. . . .

What kind of music does the person/people prefer?

. . . .

. . . .

. . . .

. . . .

What will you evaluate to recognize whether ongoing adjustments need to be made?

. . . .

. . . .

. . . .

. . . .

How many times will the piece of music be played?

. . . .

. . . .

. . . .

. . . .

Have you tested the individual/group's response to volume at a stable distance from the sound source?

. . . .

. . . .

. . . .

. . . .

Will the music be performed live or recorded, and why?

. . . .

. . . .

. . . .

. . . .

If it were as simple as answering six questions, our role as consultants would be easy. However, most people will not find it easy to identify the purpose and will assume the focus should be on the music preferences. Our role is to ask for a spread of interest across the full range of questions, and, of course, many more that emerge once the answers begin to flow.

PRINCIPLE #1: KNOWING THE PURPOSE

Throughout this book we have linked the use of different receptive methods to the needs of people who are working with a music therapist. The importance of knowing the purpose is the same in receptive music therapy as it is when using active methods such as improvisation, song writing and song recreation. Therefore, music therapists often assume that other people will understand this is the primary principle when deciding how to use music in therapy. However, many other professionals assume it is the music that has an effect on a person without understanding the importance of the therapeutic relationship and all the professional skills that are at play in that. Therefore, the need for the professional to take responsibility for decision-making is not evident to them. Even if people watch a music therapist carefully tailoring a musical experience to meet a person's evolving needs, they will focus their attention on the music, and the decision-making process will not be apparent. This is why this is our first and most important principle, and what we need to make clear to other professionals – know thy purpose!

> **CONSIDERATION #1**
> Don't do this last. Do it first! Know the purpose.

The purpose will vary enormously by context, and it is probably helpful to provide other professionals with suggestions about the kinds of goals music therapists would usually address with music. This requires us to truly embrace the transdisciplinary practice of sharing our guidelines with colleagues. If we are worried that they will no longer need us because they have our skills, this will result in poor outcomes for all involved. This is about trying to provide some basic principles, without holding anything back.

The following ideas are just examples that can be much better articulated in a specific context rather than in general statements, although they may be a useful starting point. You could add them as check boxes to the initial form, or in a dropdown menu of an electronic document.

Typical purposes in medical contexts:

- Relaxation
- Pain relief
- Distraction
- Connection to peers
- Emotional validation
- Solace
- Imaginative processes
- Issue recognition.

Typical purposes in educational contexts:

- Signalling transitions
- Accompanying daily routines
- Highlighting topics for discussion
- Relaxation
- Sensory stimulation
- Emotional processing
- Down time
- Accompanying dancing
- Background music

- Cultural representation.

Typical purposes in community contexts:

- Establishing connections with others
- Reminiscence
- Relaxation
- Supporting creative processes
- Sharing about lived experience
- Prompting discussion.

By focusing other professionals' attention on the purpose of using music listening, many of the remaining principles become logical extensions. However, if people are allowed to focus on choice of music first, which is the natural assumption, they will be lost in a stream of assumptions about what the music can do. The remaining principles help to refine their understanding of how to use the music, including the selection of what music to use.

PRINCIPLE #2: MUSIC PREFERENCES

The choice about 'what' music is the most important principle for music therapists and for other professionals to consider when using music listening. Music therapists know that people have highly divergent and unique tastes. It is almost impossible to know the kind of music someone likes without asking, although we can make educated guesses if they are not able to describe it themselves. But when it comes to choosing the music, the first question that other professionals must consider is 'What music do you like?'

CONSIDERATION #2

What music do they like? (Not you, *them*.)

Interestingly, this does not necessarily mean that the music they first describe will form the basis of the music listening experience, but it can influence both what to choose and what not to choose.

Music lovers

Some people have strong preferences for certain types of music. For example, someone might let you know that they love orchestral music but that they hate brass. Or that they love metal music and hate pop music. It is not the case for everyone, but people with strong music preferences usually have music they like, and music they don't. It is useful to understand both of these dimensions when working with people who are passionate about music.

Music likers

Some people offer quite neutral answers to the question of preferences. They may say that they like a bit of everything. Or they might say they like all music, so long as it is performed well. Sometimes this means they do like everything. Other times it means that they don't have the words to describe the type of music they like.

When people do not offer clear descriptions of their preferred music, it is possible to solicit more detail by asking them if there are specific songs they like, or particular artists, of if there is a radio station or playlist that they listen to all the time. Other helpful questions include asking about what decade they were most connected to music, or whether they have listened to music chosen by other members in their homes but which they enjoy. It might be music of their grandchildren, their parents, their partners or their friends. Even though they are not music lovers, they have noticed some types of music due to their social connections. Therefore, the question 'What kind of music do you like?' can be supplemented by further questions to get more information:

- What kind of music do you like?
- What kind of music do you dislike?
- What artists do you like?

- What bands do you like?
- Do you listen to a particular playlist or radio station?
- What years did you listen to music most?
- What kind of music do your close connections listen to?

It's not about you

What is particular about the way music therapists select music for therapeutic purposes is their pre-understanding that everyone has unique tastes. So we can draw on our own preferred music when preferences are not forthcoming, but this is not our preference. We want to know what music the people we work with like. Of course, it will be easier to source and select music if the person's preferences overlap with our own, but it is important not to sway them towards certain music preferences. The conversation should not begin with a discussion of our own preferred music. If the person politely asks, in a normal, social way, the answer should be kept brief and be quickly turned back to them for their response. When we use music in therapy, it is different to the ways we select music as the host of a party or for our own pleasure or distraction. It is *always* about them.

> **CONSIDERATION #3**
>
> Don't talk about the kind of music you like. Keep the focus on what they like.

If we feel that the person's music preferences are not well suited to the purposes that have been identified, we are left with two choices. Either adjust the purpose to better integrate the music identified – for example, changing from relaxation to emotional validation – or cautiously negotiate alternative music suggestions. If negotiating, the first conversation would be to check assumptions and to see if it is correct that the preferred music can't be used for purpose. For example, although rock music might not seem like a good match for relaxation, there are plenty of peaceful rock ballads that the person might be able to identify. If the music is meant to accompany exercise or dancing, but it doesn't have a strong rhythm, it might be possible to think of a different kind of exercise or dance that is better suited to the music.

Once music preferences have been identified, more pragmatic considerations will come into play. This often requires research to find the songs that have been nominated and if it is not the exact song or band it is useful to propose music that is similar. The remaining principles about repetition, sensitivity and live or recorded renditions will all be informed by what has been discovered in the previous principles about music preferences and the needs of the individual. This information needs to be combined to reach a decision about what music will be used in the first place, and then the ongoing monitoring and tailoring can commence.

PRINCIPLE #3: MAKE ONGOING ADJUSTMENTS

Music therapists do not necessarily follow their session plans in the ways intended. They constantly adjust and shift their intentions in response to what is happening in a session. When music is being used, the conditions are not static; they are dynamic, so people's reactions might change during a piece of music.

For example, a person might initially feel pleasantly surprised that they recognize a piece of music and respond with pleasure. Then, as it continues to play, they might have further realizations about why the music is important to them, and this may trigger a new set of emotions, whether this is grief or anger or a more complex emotional experience. These responses may continue to evolve throughout the piece, and can even continue afterwards as they reflect on it, or as it continues to play in their mind. Music doesn't just have this effect because the musical elements are changing, although they are, especially in Western classical music. It is also because of the associations that are stirred by the piece or style of music. This is just one example that is related to emotions, but it might equally be about the degree of stimulation, relaxation, pleasure, intensity or any other dimension of response.

The key point for other professionals to know is that people's responses to music can change during listening, and also between listening times. What might have been pleasurable on one day might be intolerable the next, and then pleasurable again sometime later.

> **CONSIDERATION #4**
> Responses to music are dynamic. Seek ongoing consent for listening together.

Jessica Tomlinson and John Habron (2021, p.8) describe how a range of music-based professionals can be encouraged to read the moment, which includes 'reading body language, sensing changes in emotion, and being aware of physical and verbal cues'. They describe remaining sensitive to moments when people no longer want music, and seeking ongoing consent for listening to music together. This varies significantly depending on how willing people are to communicate about their responses. As described in Chapter 5, people do not always choose to share how they are feeling as the music plays, and may instead choose to self-monitor and manage their reaction. This means that it is not always apparent that people's experiences have changed, and they no longer feel safe or comfortable.

There are many ways that music therapists monitor reactions, and these need to be learned by other professionals, particularly if the listener is not verbal. The following ideas are suggestions based on common reactions, but personally knowing the individual will help to identify changes and recognize the need for adjustments.

With non-verbal people:

- Watch for changes in the breath.
- Track eye gaze to see what is being stared at.
- Notice type and intensity of body movements.
- Observe changes in state, particularly possible seizures (musico-epilepsy).

With reserved people:

- Ask questions if you notice body movements/facial expressions.
- Prompt input at the conclusion of each piece of music.
- Use your own reaction as one way to start a discussion that will draw out their reaction.
- Use other artistic mediums, such as drawing and imagery, to process responses to music.
- Offer choices – for example, 'Would you like more, or is that enough?'

With forthcoming people:

- Listen to what they say and adjust appropriately.
- Ask insight-oriented questions to get to deeper meanings.
- Offer choices about what to do next, for example, 'Play it again, or something different?'
- Ask about what they need to listen to next.
- Remind them of purpose.

Observation is the first step and it should inform any adjustments that are made, which is the second step. The following principles outline how adjustments might be made, through the consideration of repetition, live or recorded music for listening, and also comfortable volume of the sound source. However, the most common adjustment involves processing the reaction to the music, as described in Chapter 2. If other professionals do not have training in these kinds of basic counselling skills, it is probably not appropriate for them to be using music listening in a therapeutic way, since it is common for processing to be required.

CONSIDERATION #5

Don't try to use music in a therapeutic way unless you have therapy training.

Music can easily be used for pleasure and for encouraging social connections without straying into territory that requires therapy skills. Focusing on the positive is usually a safe way to integrate music without triggering complex emotional reactions. This is how most people use music in their workplaces. They put music on to make people happy, to cheer them up, to create some energy or to cover other distressing sounds. We suggest that the following principles should still be taken into consideration in these situations, but the prior principles should only be used by those who have the professional capacity to comfortably manage emotional material and ensure that people feel safe in doing so. This is what professional training in music therapy is for.

PRINCIPLE #4: REPETITION OF THE MUSIC

One of the dimensions that needs to be considered in making adjustments is whether to play the same music again, or whether to change it. This is an important consideration that can be counterintuitive for those colleagues who are not trained in music. Some people put music on repeat in their work environment and then either forget it is playing or fail to consider how many times is suitable, based on people's reactions. Whether it is the same piece of music multiple times in one sitting, or the same music being repeated over a number of meetings, it is critical to reflect on how many times is too many. Some people will be willing and able to say when they have had enough, but many people are inclined to be polite or to trust in a professional's judgement, especially when it comes to the mysteries of music.

CONSIDERATION #6

Only repeat if it adds value, not by default.

There are a number of contexts where repetition can occur without intention, and as with all things in receptive music therapy, intentionality is critical to success. There are definitely times when more is better. If a person loves a song, they may wish to hear it every time they meet you. If a song becomes a symbol for beginning a group, it will seem strange if it is missing. If a piece of music is having the desired effect on a person's state, then repetition is the most obvious strategy rather than needlessly trying to find something that is similar. Music does not become boring if it is serving its purpose.

However, there are many times when repetition is unnecessary. Stories abound of hospital personnel leaving the same song or album playing for an entire shift as they move busily around a ward, with no time to notice or change the music. While this is easy to understand, those lying in beds have little else to focus on other than the sounds. It can become frustrating, annoying and even aggravating for people who feel trapped by the repetition of the music.

In addition, if people are not familiar with a style of music, they may not recognize that different pieces are playing because it all sounds the same. This may be the case for Western classical music, or for electronic music composed specifically for relaxation, or guitar music, but it could apply to anything. Many people cannot discern different sounds if they have not been trained to hear them. This should always be taken into account when music is being played in public spaces where people have no ability to move away or request a change. Consider the following.

In shared spaces:

- Note the reactions of different people. Some might enjoy it, but it may be torturous for others.
- Beware the unintentional repeat of a song or a playlist as it can be easy to lose track of repetitions when you are busy, but it may be the only stimulus for others.
- Consider whether music is better than silence, or not, and for whom.

Working individually:

- Assess whether the same piece of music is desired, using questions or observations of people's reactions.

- Remain dynamic – just because the music stays the same doesn't mean that you have to respond in the same way. You can be authentic in your own response each time you engage with the same piece of music.
- If people's reactions become repetitive and predictable, it may be time for something new.

CONSIDERATION #7

Unfamiliar music can all sound the same. Check in to see if it's okay.

Music can be a wonderful addition to an environment, but it is not always better than silence. Once again, it comes back to purpose. If the music is to cover other sounds such as beeping machines, or people in pain, then choose music that will be successful in masking the other sounds. Position it closer to the recipient than to the other noise source. Make sure that the volume of the music is reasonably consistent, so that the masked noises do not break through into the auditory space during quiet passages. But if it is meant to be entertaining or simulating, it will require much more attention than simply playing on repeat. Ongoing consideration will be required.

PRINCIPLE #5: SENSITIVITY TO VOLUME

Another critical area of ongoing adjustment is related to volume. Most people believe that the loudness of a piece of music is purely objective. In one way, it is. It can be measured in decibels and there are tools that can take a reading of the loudness of a space. This is critical for working in neonatology or rehabilitation when babies' or other people's cognitive development or recovery can be impaired by being over-stimulated. In these acute hospital situations, it is critical that other professionals understand the dangers of music that is too loud.

CONSIDERATION #8

Music that is too loud can do auditory and cognitive damage.

Neonatal intensive care units (NICU) are recognized as being among the most dangerous environments with regard to potential damage from music. Although the American Academy of Paediatrics has clearly recommended 45 dB (decibels) as the limit (Committee on Environmental Health 1997), there are frequent reports of this being exceeded. The environment is complex, because noises can be sudden and unexpected, but even the base level of wards can be too noisy for the at-risk infant. If working in an NICU, we recommend that music listening be used selectively, and ideally with special attention to dB levels. Music therapists working in these environments are the experts, but it can and should be monitored by all professionals.

Although less has been written about volume levels in other areas of music therapy practice, it is an important issue to consider when people are vulnerable to auditory and cognitive damage, such as when people have suffered a traumatic brain injury. Often the question of volume levels is relevant but is considered within the broader concern of overstimulation. This is one of the reasons that Principle #3 is so important, because we need to monitor people's responses to music and make ongoing adjustments. Volume is more than an issue of comfort; it is about potential damage to the brain, and must be taken seriously.

Another consideration about loudness is the distance from the speaker or the performers when the music is playing. It is one thing to stand next to the device and make a careful decision about the best volume, but the way it is experienced by the listener will be significantly impacted by their distance from the sound source. Acoustics are complex, and so the walls, roof and ceiling will all have an impact on how the sound travels across space. Similarly, if the room is sparse or densely populated this will make a difference. The quality of the speaker will also impact the quality of the sound as it travels across a space, and audio EQ (equalization) adjustments might need to be made, particularly if there is a loud bass playing (as there is in many contemporary electronic pieces), or a particularly shrill voice.

Subjective loudness

Auditory damage can be done by music that is too loud. However, there are also subjective dimensions to loudness perception that need to be taken into account in non-acute contexts. For example, people have different sensitivity to loudness. Although it might not damage their brain when the music is too loud, it can still be frustrating, distracting and even painful when music is played that is too loud for their own comfort levels. Therefore, professionals need to do an assessment of loudness sensitivity when providing music for listening.

Since music is not consistent with regard to volume, an assessment of subjective responses to volume needs is not singular; it must be ongoing. A piece of music might begin quietly but rise to a loud volume at different points in the piece. For popular music, the chorus might be louder than the verses, or for instrumental music there might be a number of swells in the volume and density of the music. Music therapists would usually know the piece of music they are playing well enough to anticipate the crescendos and diminuendos and to adjust the volume of the device as they listen together, based on their observations of the person's reactions. Ideally, anyone providing music would also be able to make these adjustments throughout the piece. However, if the music is going to be left on while the professional walks away, this needs to be considered in advance, and a good medium point needs to be found where the music is not too soft during the quiet parts of the piece, and not too loud during the peaks.

A final consideration is how the perception of sound varies depending on whether the listener chose the piece or not. Many people can cope with a high volume in the music if they selected it. However, being subjected to other people's music choices at the same volume might be experienced as painful. This is an extremely subjective, but normal, reaction from listeners, and should not be ignored as though someone is being difficult. Not all dimensions of sound sensitivity are related to decibels, and these personal responses are just as important as the neurological ones.

CONSIDERATION #9

Loudness is subjective as well as objective, and this must be taken seriously.

Once all these considerations are taken into account, careful attention to the loudness of the music being played is more complex than initially conceived. Professionals who are not trained in music therapy cannot be expected to recognize these details, and so it is important that music therapists are clear in articulating them on behalf of listeners. Even basic information about how music played at a loud volume through ear buds can be more damaging than music that travels across open spaces is an important piece of information that we should take responsibility for sharing. This will generally be accepted as a rational statement of facts, but it is also important that we advocate for the subjective experience of volume on behalf of music listeners.

PRINCIPLE #6: LIVE VERSUS RECORDED MUSIC

A final consideration about how the music will be played relates to whether a recording will be used, or if live playing would be more powerful. Again, the initial decisions about purpose will be the most important guide in making this decision. However, there are a number of other factors that need to be taken into account.

There are times when our purpose for music listening is to bring about changes in the listener's state. This might be due to agitation, pain, heightened emotionality or being in an unstable state. In these cases, if the music listening is effective it will lead to changes that occur while the music is playing. Ideally, the music could then be adjusted to meet the changing state of the listener, and this might be through changing the speed, the variability, the length or the style of the music. When playing live, this is relatively easy to do. The music-maker can slow the piece of music down, or adjust the volume, or go back to the beginning and start again without any gaps in the sound. A music therapist often does this when playing for someone who is experiencing pain and who gradually calms down and even goes to sleep. They may also do it in a context where people are agitated, so they would begin by matching the energy level in the room and then gradually change the properties of their playing in order to draw people into a more peaceful state. This is informed by a fundamental principle of music therapy practice, the iso-principle (Altschuler [1948] 2001), as described in Chapter 4.

However, non-therapy trained musicians might not instinctively take full advantage of the fact that they are producing the music. Many musicians are committed to playing the music in the way it has been recorded, or reproducing aspects of the music that are well known to fans, such as particular riffs, or building volume or speed. This is important if you are performing the music in order to connect to the associations someone has with a piece of music. This is why purpose is critical. If you are trying to have an impact on someone's state, then the approach to the performance of music needs to be much more flexible. You need to set aside stylistic expectations and focus on responding and modifying the music in the moment. Even 'Twinkle twinkle little star' can be played as a rock song, if that is what will get a child's attention.

CONSIDERATION #10

If making live music, consider adjusting the music responsively.

Another type of live music that is particularly potent and available to other professionals is using their voices to sing with therapeutic intent. Most people can sing, and it does not require additional musical training, so it can be the most accessible way of providing live music for listening in therapy. All of the other considerations apply to the voice, but there are also some that are specific to singing. Janeen Bower has outlined a number of these based on her insights into working with children who have been in coma with traumatic brain injury. In two publications on this topic (Bower and Shoemark 2012; Bower *et al.* 2014), she suggests that the singer thinks about the following.

Holding:

- Little change from the original song, with steady, metered, consistent and midlevel volume (mezzo piano–mezzo forte) singing by the music therapist.

- A simple guitar accompaniment that emphasizes the pulse of the song.

Affirming:

- A clear, legato (smooth) melody line sung by the music therapist.
- A sedate/calm singing with decreased volume (mezzo piano–piano) and tempo, muted accents and a clear legato (smooth) melody line.
- Little, or no space between the phrases of songs to provide a continuous melody line.
- A smooth guitar accompaniment (when guitar accompaniment is present), with little or no attack (sudden loud sound).

Enticing:

- An evident slowing (ritardando) in the music.
- An increased emphasis on the musical accents.
- Pauses in the song lyrics to offer space for the child to respond.
- A bright and happy vocal timbre.
- Gestural mirroring of the child's behaviours, including mirroring their breath.
- Vocal mirroring of their vocalizations.

Containing:

- A steady, clearly enunciated lyric line sung at a slow tempo and medium to loud (mezzo forte-forte) volume.
- A simplified guitar accompaniment with emphasis on the pulse of the song, such as strumming on the beat of the song to emphasize the inherent temporal organization.

These suggestions are clearly related to the vulnerable context of the listener, which necessitates a protective attitude on behalf of the performer. Bower's guidelines are designed to enhance the safety of the child, and to reduce any stimulative aspects of music sharing. They are oriented towards gentle, engaging, responsive encounters that are appropriate for an intensive care unit.

However, if the primary purpose of music listening requires the performer to reproduce a piece of music in a way that is similar to the original recording or performance, then obviously the piece should not be adjusted. This might be the case if the purpose of listening is to inspire memories, or to promote bonding between a group of people who have a shared connection to the piece. In this case, it is important that the music-maker refrains from making adjustments and is faithful to the original intentions. If a singer usually enjoys jazz interpretations of songs, they should work hard to reduce the jazz inflections in their voice and to sing in a 'straight-up' way. If they are an acoustic guitar player who enjoys acoustic versions of originals that were played by an entire band, they will need to check if that will be satisfying to the listener, who might be particularly attached to the electronic beats or the synthesized sounds. These qualities are not as important if the purpose is not connected to existing connections to the music, but they are very important if the purpose is to reproduce people's favourite songs.

CONSIDERATION #11

Assess whether the original production of the music is important to the listener.

The final considerations are related to the performer. As noted, there can be excellent reasons to use live music to address the purpose of music listening. None of these is related to the experience of the performer. Although music therapists are all professional musicians, a foundational premise of training is that sharing music is not driven by the therapist's music preferences. Music can be a powerful way of bringing about therapeutic change, but, like all therapy, this requires a complete focus on the needs of the person who is supposed to benefit from music listening. There are many wonderful musicians who perform live music in hospitals, schools and community contexts for the enjoyment of an audience. However, music listening in a therapeutic context is different. It is not about enjoyment and appreciation of the performer, composer or producer. These guidelines are not necessarily relevant for public performances, which have different considerations.

CONSIDERATION #12

Music listening for therapeutic purpose is different to music performing for an audience.

Although this is not the purpose of these guidelines, music therapists have also developed guidelines for performers working in organizations with vulnerable people. Helen Shoemark (2009) developed guidelines for musicians playing in hospitals based on her careful analysis of what musicians, patients, families and professionals needed during a pilot programme in a children's hospital. She drew on Deanna Hanson-Abromeit's work for music selection criteria (2006), and added additional, insightful criteria for the performers (see Appendix 2 of her publication).

Key questions that other professionals might use when making decisions about whether to play music that is pre-recorded or to perform it live should be based on the purpose of the music:

- Is the purpose to connect to memories of the original song? If yes, play a recording of the original song.
- Is the purpose to effect a change in a person or group state? If yes, consider using live music that is carefully adjusted using the iso-principle.
- Does the performer have enough sensitivity and musical capacity to make adjustments to the song in response to what is observed in how people are reacting? If not, do not use live music in a context where vulnerable people might be impacted.

CONCLUSION

This book has provided a detailed exploration of receptive music therapy methods, both the specific methods that are used and the broader principles that inform its use. This final chapter has provided a synthesis of this information, reconceived as a set of principles and considerations that might be useful for explaining the ways we use music in therapy to other professionals and carers.

Receptive music therapy is more than music listening; it is the embedding of shared listening in the context of a therapeutic process and relationship. It can be poignant, and is often emotional, and usefully, it can be readily practised online as well as in real-life contexts. Receptive music therapy methods have become more prominent in recent times because of technological developments and a rapidly expanded access to recorded music. We believe it is a most satisfying and powerful way to work with people in practice contexts, and that new methods will continue to emerge over the coming years.

References

Aadal, L., Hald, S.V., Setterberg, U.J. and Bonde, L.O. (2021) 'Music listening to decrease intensity of agitated behaviour after severe acquired brain injury: An exploratory multi-case study.' *Music & Medicine 13*(1), 68–76.

Aasgaard, T. (2001) 'An ecology of love: Aspects of music therapy in the pediatric oncology environment.' *Journal of Palliative Care 17*(3), 177.

Altschuler, I.M. (1944) 'Four years experience with music as a therapeutic agent at Eloise Hospital.' *American Journal of Psychiatry, 100*(7), 792–794. Available at: https://doi.org/10.1176/ajp.100.7.792

Altschuler, I.M. ([1948] 2001) 'A psychiatrist's experience with music as a therapeutic agent.' *Nordic Journal of Music Therapy 10*(1), 69–76. Available at: https://doi.org/10.1080/08098130109478019

Amir, D. (2012) '"My music is me": Musical presentation as a way of forming and sharing identity in music therapy group.' *Nordic Journal of Music Therapy 21*(2), 176–193.

Archambault, K., Vaugon, K., Deumie, V., Brault, M., Perez, R. and Peyrin, J. (2019) 'MAP: A personalised receptive music therapy intervention to improve the affective well-being of youths hospitalised in a mental health unit.' *Journal of Music Therapy 56*(4), 381–402.

Armstrong, B.J., Dirnt, M. and Cool, T. (1997) 'Time of your life' ('Good riddance') [Song recorded by Green Day]. *Nimrod*. Reprise Records.

Batt-Rawden, K.B., DeNora, T. and Ruud, E. (2005) 'Music listening and empowerment in health promotion: A study of the role and significance of music in everyday life of the long-term ill.' *Nordic Journal of Music Therapy 14*(2), 120–136. Available at: https://doi.org/10.1080/08098130509478134

Baumel, L. (1973) 'Psychiatrist as music therapist.' *Journal of Music Therapy 10*, 83–85.

Beck, B.D., Messel, C., Meyer, S.L., Cordtz, T.O., *et al.* (2018) 'Feasibility of trauma-focused Guided Imagery and Music with adult refugees diagnosed with PTSD: A pilot study.' *Nordic Journal of Music Therapy 27*(1), 67–86.

Bensimon, M., Bodner, E. and Shrira, A. (2017) 'The emotional impact of national music on young and older adults differing in posttraumatic stress disorder symptoms.' *Aging & Mental Health 21*(10), 1090–1098.

Bergström-Isacsson, M. (2012) 'And what about the experience of the music? A response to Jeff Hooper's article.' *Australian Journal of Music Therapy 23*, 73–74.

Bibb, J. and McFerran, K.S. (2018) 'Musical recovery: The role of group singing in regaining healthy relationships with music to promote mental health recovery.' *Nordic Journal of Music Therapy 27*(3). Available at: https://doi.org/10.1080/08098131.2018.1432676

Biswas, A. (2011) 'The music of what happens.' In D. Clarke and E. Clark (eds) *Music and Consciousness: Philosophical, Psychological, and Cultural Perspectives* (pp.95–110). Oxford: Oxford University Press.

Bonde, L.O. (2005) 'The Bonny Method of Guided Imagery and Music (BMGIM) with cancer survivors. A psychosocial study with focus on the influence of BMGIM on mood and quality of life' [PhD dissertation]. Aalborg University, Denmark.

Bonny, H. (2002) *Music and consciousness*. Gilsum, NH: Barcelona.

Booth, J. (2005–06) 'Music, drawing and narrative: An adaptation of the Bonny Method of Guided Imagery and Music.' *Journal of the Association for Music and Imagery 10*, 55–73.

Bower, J. and Shoemark, H. (2012) 'Music therapy for the pediatric patient experiencing agitation during post-traumatic amnesia: Constructing a foundation from theory.' *Music & Medicine 4*(3), 146–152.

Bower, J., Catroppa, C., Grocke, D. and Shoemark, S. (2014) 'Music therapy for early cognitive rehabilitation post childhood TBI: An intrinsic mixed methods case study.' *Developmental Rehabilitation 17*(5), 339–346.

Bradt, J., Dileo, C. and Potvin, N. (2013) 'Music for stress and anxiety reduction in coronary heart disease patients.' *Cochrane Database of Systematic Reviews 12*, CD006577.

Branch, M. and Shanks, J. (2003) 'Are you happy now?' [Song recorded by Michelle Branch]. *Hotel Paper*. Maverick/Warner Australia.

Brock, M. and Hsu, M. (2005) 'Courage' [Song recorded by Superchick]. *Beauty from Pain*. Inpop Records.

Brooks, D. (1989) 'Music therapy enhances treatment with adolescents.' *Music Therapy Perspectives 6*, 37–39.

Bruscia, K.E. (1998a) *Defining Music Therapy* (2nd edn). Gilsum, NH: Barcelona Publishers.

Bruscia, K.E. (1998b) *The Dynamics of Music Psychotherapy*. Gilsum, NH: Barcelona Publishers.

Bruscia, K.E. (2014) *Defining Music Therapy* (3rd edn). Dallas, TX: Barcelona Publishers.

Burns, D., Meadows, A., Althouse, S., Perkins, S. and Cripe, L. (2018) 'Differences between supportive music imagery and music listening during outpatient chemotherapy and potential moderators of treatment effects.' *Journal of Music Therapy 55*(1), 83–108.

Burrai, F., Sanna, G., Moccia, E., Morlando, F., *et al.* (2020) 'Beneficial effects of listening to classical music in patients with heart failure.' *Journal of Cardiac Failure 26*(7), 541–549.

Butler, B. (1966) 'Music group psychotherapy.' *Journal of Music Therapy 3*(2), 53–56.

Cannon, J.W. and Greasley, A.E. (2021) 'Exploring relationships between electronic dance music event participation and well-being.' *Music and Science 4*. doi:10.1177/2059204321997102.

Cepeda, M.S., Carr, D.B., Lau, J. and Alvarez, H. (2006) 'Music for pain relief.' *Cochrane Database of Systematic Reviews 2*, CD004843.

Chan, M.F., Wong, Z.Y. and Thayala, N.V. (2010) 'A systematic review on the effectiveness of music listening in reducing depressive symptoms in adults.' *JBI Library of Systematic Reviews 8*(31), 1242–1287.

Chang, J. (2007) *Can't Stop Won't Stop: A History of the Hip-Hop Generation*. New York: St Martin's Press.

Cheong-Clinch, C. (2019) 'My iPod, YouTube, and our playlists: Connections made in and beyond therapy.' In K.S. McFerran, P. Derrington and S. Saarikallio (eds) *Handbook of Music, Adolescents, and Wellbeing* (pp.225–236). Oxford: Oxford University Press.

Cheong-Clinch, C. and McFerran, K.S. (2016) `Musical diaries: Examining the daily preferred music listening of Australian young people with mental illness.' *Journal of Applied Youth Studies 1*(2), 77–94.

Chodorow, J. (1997) *Jung on Active Imagination*. Abingdon: Routledge.

Clark, D. and Kini, T. (2011) 'North Indian classical music and its links with consciousness: The case of dhrupad.' In D. Clark and E. Clark (eds) *Music and Consciousness: Philosophical, Psychological, and Cultural Perspectives* (pp.137–156). Oxford: Oxford University Press.

Clark, I.N., Baker, F.A. and Taylor, N.F. (2016) 'Older adults' music listening preferences to support physical activity following cardiac rehabilitation.' *Journal of Music Therapy 53*(4), 364–397. Available at: https://doi.org/10.1093/jmt/thw011

Committee on Environmental Health (1997) 'Noise: A hazard for the fetus and newborn.' *Pediatrics 100*(4), 724–727.

Copland, A. (1953) *What to Listen for in Music*. London: Penguin Books.

Crenshaw, K. (1991) 'Mapping the margins: Intersectionality, identity politics, and violence against women of color.' *Stanford Law Review 43*(6), 1241–1299.

Csikszentmihalyi, M. (2002) *Flow: The Classic Work on How to Achieve Happiness*. London: Rider (Random House).

DeNora, T. (2021) Book Review Essay, 'Can music fight disease? Can cultural sociology help? Norwegian vistas.' *Contemporary Sociology 50*(5), 384–391.

de Witte, M., Spruit, A., van Hooren, S., Moonen, X. and Stams, G.J. (2020a) 'Effects of music interventions on stress-related outcomes: A systematic review and two meta-analyses.' *Health Psychology Review 14*(2), 294–324. Available at: https://doi.org/10.1080/17437199.2019.1627897

de Witte, M., da Silva Pinho, A., Stams, G.-J., Moonen, X., Bos, A. and van Hooren, S. (2020b) 'Music therapy for stress reduction: A systematic review and meta-analysis.' *Health Psychology Review 27*, 1–26. doi:10.1080/17437199.2020.1846580.

Díaz de Chumaceiro, C.L. (1992) 'What song comes to mind? Induced song recall: Transference/countertransference in dyadic music associations in treatment and supervision.' *The Arts in Psychotherapy 19*(5), 325–332.

Dileo, C. (1989) 'A comprehensive definition of music therapy with an integrative model for music medicine.' In R. Spintge and R. Droh (eds) *Music Medicine* (pp.19–29). St Louis, MO: MMB Music.

Dimiceli-Mitran, L. (2020) 'Focused Music Imagery (FMI): Pathway through the psyche.' *Journal of the Association for Music and Imagery 17*, 37–54.

Duckworth, K., Williams, P. and Spears, M. (2015) 'Alright' [Song recorded by Kendrick Lamar]. *To Pimp a Butterfly*. Top Dawg/Aftermath/Interscope.

Duncan, B.L., Miller, S.D. and Sparks, J. (2004) *The Heroic Client: A Revolutionary Way to Improve Effectiveness through Client-Directed, Outcome-Informed Therapy.* San Francisco, CA: Jossey-Bass.

Dylan, B. (1963) 'Blowin' in the wind' [Song recorded by Bob Dylan]. *The Freewheelin' Bob Dylan*. Columbia Records.

Dvorak, A. (2017) 'A conceptual framework for group processing of lyric analysis interventions in music therapy mental health practice.' *Music Therapy Perspectives 35*(2), 190–198. doi:10.1093/mtp/miw032.

Egan, G. (1998) *The Skilled Helper* (6th edn). Pacific Grove, CA: Brooks-Cole.

Einstein, A. ([1931] 2009) *Einstein on Cosmic Religion and Other Opinions and Aphorisms*. New York: Dover Publications.

Erdonmez, D. [Grocke] (1977) 'Music as a projective technique.' *Proceedings of the Third Annual Conference of the Australian Music Therapy Association*, Adelaide, pp.11–17.

Fidler, H. and Miksza, P. (2020) 'Music interventions and pain: An integrative review and analysis of recent literature.' *Approaches: An Interdisciplinary Journal of Music Therapy 12*(1), 43–71.

Fiore, J. (2018) 'A pilot study exploring the use of an online pre-composed receptive music experience for students coping with stress and anxiety.' *Journal of Music Therapy 55*(4), 383–407.

Flynn, L. (2014) 'The stories we haven't told: The lived experience of music used in therapy for bereaved parents' [Doctoral thesis]. The University of Queensland, Australia.

Freud, S. ([1924] 1956) *A General Introduction to Psychoanalysis*. New York: Washington Square Press.

Freud, S. (1966) 'Hysteria.' In *The Standard Edition of the Complete Psychological Works of Sigmund Freud, Volume I (1886–1899): Pre-Psycho-Analytic Publications and Unpublished Drafts* (pp.37–59). London: Hogarth Press.

Gabrielsson, A. (2001) 'Emotions in strong experiences with music.' In P.N Juslin and J.A. Sloboda (eds) *Music and Emotion: Theory and Research* (pp.431–449). Series in Affective Science. Oxford: Oxford University Press.

Gabrielsson, A. (2011) 'Strong experiences with music.' In P.N. Juslin and J.A. Sloboda (eds) *Handbook of Music and Emotion: Theory, Research, Applications* (pp.547–574). Oxford: Oxford University Press.

Gallagher, L.M., Lagman, R. and Rybicki, L. (2018) 'Outcomes of music therapy interventions on symptom management in palliative medicine patients.' *American Journal of Hospice and Palliative Medicine 35*(2), 250–257.

Gardstrom, S. and Hiller, J. (2010) 'Song discussion as music psychotherapy.' *Music Therapy Perspectives 28*(2), 147–156.

Geipel, J. (2019) 'Between down in the dumps and over the moon: Music therapy for young people with depression.' In K.S. McFerran, P. Derrington and S. Saarikallio (eds) *Handbook of Music, Adolescents, and Wellbeing* (pp.53–64). Oxford: Oxford University Press.

George, N. (2005) *Hip Hop America*. New York: Penguin Books.

Germer, C.K., Fulton, P.R. and Siegel, R.D. (eds) (2016). *Mindfulness and Psychotherapy* (2nd edn). New York: Guilford Press.

Ghent, E. (1990) 'Masochism, submission, surrender – Masochism as a perversion of surrender.' In S.A. Mitchell and L. Aron (eds) *Relational Psychoanalysis: The Emergence of the Tradition* (pp.211–242). London: The Analytic Press.

Ghetti, C. (2012) 'Music therapy as procedural support for invasive medical procedures: Toward the development of music therapy theory.' *Nordic Journal of Music Therapy 21*(1), 3–35.

Gilboa, A. and Salman, B. (2019) 'The roles of music in Let's talk music, a model for enhancing communication between Arabs and Jews in Israel.' *Nordic Journal of Music Therapy 28*(3), 256–268.

Gilboa, A., Yehuda, N. and Amir, D. (2009) 'Let's talk music: A musical-communal project for enhancing communication among students of multi-cultural origin.' *Nordic Journal of Music Therapy 18*(1), 3–31.

Gimeno, M. (2015) 'MED-GIM adaptations of the Bonny Method for medical patients: Individual sessions.' In D. Grocke and T. Moe (eds) *Guided Imagery & Music (GIM) and Music Imagery Methods for Individual and Group Therapy* (pp.179–187). London: Jessica Kingsley Publishers.

Giordano, F., Scarlata, E., Baroni, M., Gentile, E., *et al.* (2020) 'Receptive music therapy to reduce stress and improve wellbeing in Italian clinical staff involved in COVID-19 pandemic: A preliminary study.' *The Arts in Psychotherapy 70*, 101689.

Gold, C., Rolvsjord, R., Mössler, K. and Stige, B. (2013) 'Reliability and validity of a scale to measure interest in music among clients in mental health care.' *Psychology of Music 41*(5), 665–682.

Grocke, D. (2014) 'Imagery.' In W.F. Thompson (ed.) *Music in the Social and Behavioral Sciences: An Encyclopedia* (pp.577–581). Thousand Oaks, CA: SAGE Publications Ltd.

Grocke, D.E. (ed.) (2019) *Guided Imagery and Music: The Bonny Method and Beyond* (2nd edn). Gilsum, NH: Barcelona Publishers.

Grocke, D. and Wigram, T. (2007) *Receptive Methods in Music Therapy*. London: Jessica Kingsley Publishers.

Hanning, B. (2002) *Concise History of Western Music* (2nd edn). New York: W.W. Norton & Co.

Hanser, S. (1990) 'A music therapy strategy for depressed older adults in the community.' *Journal of Applied Gerontology* 9(3), 283–298.

Hanson-Abromeit, D. (2006) 'Developmentally based criteria to support recorded music selections by neonatal nurses for use with premature infants in the neonatal intensive care unit' [Dissertation abstract]. *Dissertation Abstracts International Section A: Humanities and Social Sciences 67*(4-A), 1143.

Heiderscheit, A. and Madson, A. (2015) 'Use of the iso principle as a central method in mood management: A music psychotherapy clinical case study.' *Music Therapy Perspectives 33*(1), 42–52.

Hense, C. and McFerran, K.S. (2017) 'Promoting young people's musical identities to facilitate recovery from mental illness.' *Journal of Youth Studies 20*(8), 997–1012. Available at: https://doi.org/10.1080/13676261.2017.1287888

Hense, C., McFerran, K.S. and McGorry, P. (2014) 'Constructing a grounded theory of young people's recovery of musical identity in mental illness.' *The Arts in Psychotherapy 41*, 594–603.

Hense, C., McFerran, K.S. and Silverman, M.J. (2018) 'Using the healthy–unhealthy uses of music scale as a single session music therapy intervention on an acute youth mental health inpatient unit.' *Music Therapy Perspectives 36*(2), 267–276.

Herman, J. (1992) *Trauma and Recovery: The Aftermath of Violence*. New York: Basic Books.

Hooper, J. (2012) 'Predictable Factors in Sedative Music (PFSM): A tool to identify sedative music for receptive music therapy.' *Australian Journal of Music Therapy 23*, 59–74.

Howlin, C. and Rooney, B. (2020) 'The cognitive mechanisms in music listening interventions for pain: A scoping review.' *Journal of Music Therapy* 57(2), 127–167. doi:10.1093/jmt/thaa003.

Jacobson, E. (1938) *Progressive Relaxation: A Physiological and Clinical Investigation of Muscular States and Their Significance in Psychology and Medical Practice*. Chicago, IL: University of Chicago Press.

Jespersen, K.V. and Vuust, P. (2012) 'The effect of relaxation music listening on sleep quality in traumatized refugees: A pilot study.' *Journal of Music Therapy 49*(2), 205–229.

Jespersen, K.V., Madsen, J. and Vuust, P. (2020) 'Bedtime music for sleep problems in older adults with dementia: A feasibility study.' *Music & Medicine 12*(4), 222–230.

Jiang, J., Zhou, L., Rickson, D. and Jiang, C. (2013) 'The effects of sedative and stimulative music on stress reduction depend on music preference.' *The Arts in Psychotherapy 40*, 201–205.

Jung, C. (1959) *The Archetypes and the Collective Unconscious* (2nd edn). London: Routledge.

Kabat-Zinn, J. (2005) *Coming to Our Senses.* New York: Hyperion.

Kees, N.L. and Jacobs, E. (1990) 'Working with groups: Conducting more effective groups: How to select and process group exercises.' *Journal for Specialists in Group Work 15*(1), 21–29.

Kern, P. and Tague, D. (2017) 'Music therapy practice status and trends worldwide: An international survey study.' *Journal of Music Therapy 54*(3), 255–286.

Körlin, D. (2019) 'Music breathing.' In D. Grocke (ed.) *Guided Imagery and Music: The Bonny Method and Beyond* (2nd edn) (pp.531–560). New Braunfels, TX: Barcelona Publishers.

Krout, R. (2007) 'Music listening to facilitate relaxation and promote wellness: Integrated aspects of our neurophysiological responses to music.' *The Arts in Psychotherapy 34*, 134–141.

Lecourt, E. (1998) 'The role of aesthetics in countertransference: A comparison of active versus receptive music therapy.' In K. Bruscia (ed.) *The Dynamics of Music Psychotherapy* (pp.299–314). Gilsum, NH: Barcelona Publishers.

Lee, J.H. (2016) 'The effects of music on pain: A meta analysis.' *Journal of Music Therapy 53*(4), 430–477.

Lee-Harris, G., Timmers, R., Humberstone, N. and Blackburn, D. (2018) 'Music for relaxation: A comparison across two age groups.' *Journal of Music Therapy 55*(4), 439–462.

Lie, J. (2015) *K-Pop: Popular Music, Cultural Amnesia, and Economic Innovation in South Korea.* Berkeley, CA: University of California Press.

Long, E. (2016) 'Effect of a personalized music playlist on a patient with dementia and evening agitation.' *Annals of Long Term Care 24*(11), 31–33.

Lund, H., Bertelsen, L. and Bonde, L.O. (2016) 'Sound and music interventions in psychiatry at Aalborg University Hospital.' *SoundEffects – An Interdisciplinary Journal of Sound and Sound Experience 6*(1), 48–68. Available at: https://doi.org/10.7146/se.v6i1.24912

Mårtenson Blom, K. (2011) 'Transpersonal-spiritual BMGIM experiences and the process of surrender.' *Nordic Journal of Music Therapy 20*(2), 185–203. doi:10.1080/08098131.2010.48764.

McFerran, K.S. and Saarikallio, S. (2013) 'Depending on music to make me feel better: Who is responsible for the ways young people appropriate music for health benefits.' *The Arts in Psychotherapy 41*(1), 89–97.

McFerran, K.S., Derrington, P. and Saarikallio, S. (eds) (2019) *Handbook of Music, Adolescents, and Wellbeing.* Oxford: Oxford University Press.

McFerran, K.S., Hense, C., Koike, A. and Rickwood, D. (2018) 'Intentional music use to reduce psychological distress in adolescents accessing primary mental health care.' *Clinical Child Psychology and Psychiatry 23*(4), 567–581. doi:10.1177/1359104518767231.

McLeod, K. (2001) 'Genres, subgenres, sub-subgenres and more: Musical and social differentiation within electronic/dance music communities.' *Journal of Popular Music Studies 13*(1), 59–75.

Medcalf, L. (2016) 'Musical intimacy and the negotiation of boundary challenges in contemporary music therapy practice' [Doctoral thesis]. Faculty of Fine Arts and Music, University of Melbourne, Australia.

Melzack, R. and Wall, P.D. (1965) 'Pain mechanisms. A new theory.' *Science 150*, 971–978.

Melzack, R. and Katz, J. (2004) 'The gate control theory: reaching for the brain.' In T. Hadjistavroploulos and K.D. Craig (Eds.), *Pain: Psychological Perspectives*, pp.13–34. Mahwah, NJ: Lawrence Erlbaum Associates.

Mena, M. and Solvang, A. (2008) 'Eyesore' [Song recorded by Maria Mena]. *Cause and Effect*. Sony Music/Columbia.

Ng, R. (2015) 'Chinese music programme: Harvest.' In D. Grocke and T. Moe (eds) *Guided Imagery & Music (GIM) and Music Imagery Methods for Individual and Group Therapy* (pp.319–328). London: Jessica Kingsley Publishers.

Ng, R. (2018) 'The application of the Chinese Yin–Yang concept and Chinese music in Guided Imagery and Music' [PhD dissertation]. University of Melbourne, Australia. Available at: http://hdl.handle.net/11343/215896

Nolan, P. (2005) 'Verbal processing within the music therapy relationship.' *Music Therapy Perspectives 23*(1), 18–28.

North, A.C., Hargreaves, D.J. and O'Neill, S.A. (2000) 'The importance of music to adolescents.' *British Journal of Educational Psychology 70*(2), 255–272.

O'Callaghan, C. (1984) 'Musical profiles of dying patients.' Bulletin, Australian Music Therapy Association, 5–11 June.

Ogden, P., Minton, K. and Pain, C. (2006) *Trauma and the Body: A Sensorimotor Approach to Psychotherapy.* Norton Series on Interpersonal Neurobiology. New York: W.W. Norton & Co.

Park, J.-S. and Yoo, G.-H. (2012) 'Gangnam style' [Song recorded by Psy]. *Psy6 (6 Rules)*. YG/Universal Republic/School Boy.

Pasiali, V., Quick, D., Hassall, J. and Park, H. (2020) 'Music therapy programming for persons with eating disorders.' *Voices: A World Forum for Music Therapy 20*(3). Available at: https://doi.org/10.15845/voices.v20i3.2785

Pauker, S.G. and Wong, J.B. (2005) 'The influence of influence diagrams in medicine.' *Decision Analysis, INFORMS 2*(4), 238–244.

Pelletier, C. (2004) 'The effect of music on decreasing arousal due to stress: A meta-analysis.' *Journal of Music Therapy 41*(3), 192–214.

Perry, B., Buck, P., Mills, M. and Stipe, M. (1985) 'Can't get there from here' [Song recorded by R.E.M.]. *Fables of the Reconstruction*. IRS Records.

Pinkerton, J.A. and Duggan, R.A. (2020) *Method and System for Influencing Emotional Regulation through Assessment, Education, and Music Playlist Applications* (USA Patent No. 16/666,378).

Ray, K.D. and Fitzsimmons, S. (2014) 'Music-assisted bathing: Making shower time easier for people with dementia.' *Journal of Gerontological Nursing* 40(2), 9–13.

Reher, M. (2015) 'Guided Imagery and Music with children: Exploration of loss from a young age.' In D. Grocke and T. Moe (eds) *Guided Imagery & Music (GIM) and Music Imagery Methods for Individual and Group Therapy* (pp.178–188). London: Jessica Kingsley Publishers.

Reik, T. (1953) *The Haunting Melody: Psychoanalytic Experiences in Life and Music*. New York: Farrar, Straus & Young.

Robb, S.L. (2000) 'Music-assisted progressive muscle relaxation, music listening, and silence. A comparison of relaxation techniques.' *Journal of Music Therapy* 37(1), 2–21.

Rogers, C. (1951) *Client-Centered Therapy: Its Current Practice, Implications and Theory*. London: Constable.

Rolvsjord, R. (2010) *Resource Oriented Music Therapy*. Gilsum, NH: Barcelona Publishers.

Rose, T. (1994) *Black Noise: Rap Music and Black Culture in Contemporary America* (Vol. 6). Hanover, NH: Wesleyan University Press.

Rose, T. (2008) *The Hip Hop Wars: What We Talk About When We Talk About Hip Hop – and Why It Matters*. New York: Basic/Civitas Books.

Rudstam, G., Elofsson, U., Søndergaard, H.P., Bonde, L.O. and Beck, B.D. (2017) 'Trauma-focused group music and imagery with women suffering from PTSD/complex PTSD.' *Approaches* 9, 202–216.

Ruud, E. (1997) 'Music and identity.' *Nordic Journal of Music Therapy* 6(1), 3–13.

Ruud, E. (2002) 'Music as a cultural immunogen: Three narratives on the use of music as a technology of health.' In I.M. Hanken, S.G. Nielsen and M. Nerland (eds) *Research in and for Higher Music Education. Festschrift for Harald Jergensen* (pp.109–120). Oslo: Norwegian Academy of Music.

Saarikallio, S., McFerran, K.S. and Gold, C. (2015) 'Development and validation of the Healthy–Unhealthy Music Scale (HUMS).' *Child and Adolescent Mental Health* 20(4), 210–217.

Salmon, D. (1989) 'Partage: Group-work in palliative care.' In *The Next Step Forward: Music Therapy with the Terminally Ill, Proceedings from a Symposium for Music Therapists Working in Palliative Care.* (pp.47–52) Bronx, NY: Calvary Hospital.

Schwartz, E.K. (2019) *Basic Verbal Skills for Music Therapists*. Gilsum, NH: Barcelona Publishers.

Scott, T. (1964) *Music for Zen Meditation*. Verve.

Scott-Moncrieff, S. (2019) 'Listening deeply: Using music and imagery in self-care' [Conference presentation]. Music and Imagery Association of Australia Conference, Melbourne.

Scott-Moncrieff, S., Beck, B. and Montgomery, E. (2015) 'North American conference highlights the treatment of trauma utilising Guided Imagery and Music.' *Music & Medicine* 7, 72–75.

Shin, H. (2009) 'Have you ever seen the Rain? And who'll stop the Rain? The globalizing project of Korean pop (K-pop).' *Inter-Asia Cultural Studies 10*(4), 507–523.

Shoemark, H. (2009) 'Sweet melodies: Combining the talents and knowledge of music therapy and elite musicianship.' *Voices: A World Forum for Music Therapy 9*(2). Available at: https://voices.no/index.php/voices/article/view/1819/1582

Shoemark, H., Hanson-Abromeit, D. and Stewart, L. (2015) 'Constructing optimal experience for the hospitalized newborn through neuro-based music therapy.' *Frontiers in Human Neuroscience 9*, 487.

Short, A. and Ahern, N. (2009) 'Evaluation of a systematic development process: Relaxing music for the emergency department.' *Australian Journal of Music Therapy 20*(1), 3–26.

Siegel, D.J. (1999) *The Developing Mind: Toward a Neurobiology of Interpersonal Experience.* New York: Guilford Press.

Skänland, M.S. (2011) 'Use of Mp3-players as a coping resource.' *Music and Arts in Action 3*(2), 15–33.

Small, C. (1998) *Musicking: The Meanings of Performing and Listening*. Middletown, CT: Wesleyan University Press.

Smith, M. (2008) 'The effects of a single music relaxation session on state anxiety levels of adults in a workplace environment.' *Australian Journal of Music Therapy 19*, 45–66.

Spielberger, C.D. (1983) *Manual for the State–Trait Anxiety Inventory*. Palo Alto, CA: Consulting Psychologists Press.

Summer, L. (2009) 'Client perspectives on the music in GIM' [PhD dissertation]. Aalborg University, Denmark. Available at: https://vbn.aau.dk/ws/portalfiles/portal/316409760/6467_lisa_summer_thesis.pdf

Summer, L. (2012) 'Case examples of levels of Guided Imagery and Music (GIM) therapy: The evolution of a continuum.' In K. Bruscia (ed.) *Case Examples of Guided Imagery and Music* (pp.209–214). Gilsum, NH: Barcelona Publishers.

Summer, L. (2015) 'The journey of Guided Imagery and Music (GIM) training from self-exploration to a continuum of clinical practice.' In D. Grocke and T. Moe (eds) *Guided Imagery & Music (GIM) and Music Imagery Methods for Individual and Group Therapy* (pp.339–348). London: Jessica Kingsley Publishers.

Summer, L. (2019) 'Group music and imagery therapy.' In D. Grocke (ed.) *Guided Imagery and Music: The Bonny Method and Beyond* (2nd edn) (pp.259–266). Gilsum, NH: Barcelona Publishers.

Swift, T. and Martin, M. (2012) 'We are never ever getting back together' [Song recorded by Taylor Swift]. *Red*. Big Machine Records.

Tan, X., Yowler, C., Super, D. and Fratianne, R. (2012) 'The interplay of preference, familiarity and psychophysical properties in defining relaxing music.' *Journal of Music Therapy 49*(2), 15–179.

Tanhane, A. (2020) 'How does a critical analysis of the literature inform recommendations for writing about mindfulness in music therapy practice?' [Master's thesis]. University of Melbourne, Australia.

Taylor, N. and Dallas, D. (1967) 'I wish I knew how it would feel to be free' [Song recorded by Nina Simone]. *Silk and Soul*. RCA Records.

Thompson, S. (2011) 'The impact and effect of group music therapy on anxiety, depression, quality of life and coping with women with breast cancer: A mixed methods study' [PhD thesis]. Faculty of Music, University of Melbourne, Australia. Available at: http://cat.lib.unimelb.edu.au/record=b4133387

Tomlinson, J. and Habron, J. (2021) 'How music-for-health practitioners' decision-making processes inform their practice in paediatric hospitals.' *Approaches: An Interdisciplinary Journal of Music Therapy* [online first]. Available at: http://approaches.gr/tomlinson-a20210205

Travis Jr, R. (2015) *The Healing Power of Hip Hop*. Westport, CT: Praeger.

van Dort, C. and Grocke, D. (2014) 'Music, imagery and mindfulness in substance dependency.' In L. Rappaport (ed.) *Mindfulness and the Arts Therapies* (pp.117–128). London: Jessica Kingsley Publishers.

Wadge, A., Sheeran, E. and Labrinth (2017) 'Save myself.' *Divide*. Asylum/Atlantic Records.

Wagner, E., Lee, H. and Mason, D. (2016) 'The effect of a personal playlist on older adults with dementia.' *The Advanced Generalist: Social Work Research Journal 2*(1), 14–27.

Wärja, M. (2015) 'KMR (Short Music Journeys) with women recovering from gynecological cancer.' In D. Grocke and T. Moe (eds) *Guided Imagery & Music (GIM) and Music Imagery Methods for Individual and Group Therapy* (pp.253–266). London: Jessica Kingsley Publishers.

Wärja, M. and Bonde, L.O. (2014) 'Music as co-therapist: Towards a taxonomy of music in therapeutic music and imagery work.' *Music & Medicine 6*(2), 16–27.

Wheeler, B.L. (1983) 'A psychotherapeutic classification of music therapy practices: A continuum of procedures.' *Music Therapy Perspectives 1*(2), 8–12.

Wigram, T. (2004) *Improvisation: Methods and Techniques for Music Therapy Clinicians, Educators and Students*. London: Jessica Kingsley Publishers.

Wooten, M.A. (1992) 'The effects of heavy metal music on affects shifts of adolescents in an inpatient psychiatric setting.' *Music Therapy Perspectives 10*(2), 93–98.

Yalom, I. (1970) *The Theory and Practice of Group Psychotherapy* (3rd edn). New York: Basic Books.

Appendix A

Relaxation Induction Scripts

SHORT RELAXATION

The focus here can be on releasing any tension, or tiredness, or pain – choose one of these words, or another word, and use it consistently.

The script

> First of all, take a few moments to get as comfortable as possible in the chair [or on the bed]. As you get comfortable allow your body to be balanced...with your feet on the floor [if in a chair], feet gently resting [if in bed], arms either in your lap or loosely at each side... And now feel the support of the chair [or bed] for your neck...shoulders...back...hips...and under the legs. Allow your body to sink into the chair [or bed], knowing you are physically supported...allow your eyes to close gently... And now become aware of your breathing. Just notice the breath...the cycle of taking in the breath and releasing it... Notice how the chest and stomach rise as you breathe in, and fall as you breathe out... Take in a deep breath and gently allow the breath to be released, feeling any tension/tiredness/pain to flow out of the body.

Repeat the phrase 'Taking in a deep breath and gently releasing any tension/tiredness/pain' (choose one of these), for each statement:

> ...from the neck and shoulders [pause]

...from the arms and hands [pause]

...from the chest and stomach [pause]

...from the back, particularly the lower back [pause]

...from the hips [pause]

...from the legs [pause]

...from the feet [pause]

...the face...through the forehead, cheeks and jaw [pause]

Adding music:

And now allow the music to flow through your body (and bring comfort). [Start the music]

Or for supportive music imagery (see Chapter 7):

Bringing to your mind the image of the...[the image has been worked out before the beginning of the script]. Notice the colour and shape of the image and what the image brings to you...and allow the music to be with the image.

End of music:

Stay with the relaxed feeling, knowing you can return to this restful state again...begin to become aware of your body...gently stretch your legs and your arms...take in a deep breath and release it...[the therapist can model this audibly]...give your body a big stretch [the therapist can model this stretch, including the audible breathing].

STEP-BY-STEP STRUCTURED/ COUNT-DOWN RELAXATION INDUCTION

Some clients prefer an induction that they can follow easily. This step-by-step structured induction is suitable for clients who are tired or confused (for example, people who have mental illness, or in early-stage dementia). This version of the count-down technique is only from 5–1 to induce relaxation, and then 1–5 to return to an alert state. It can be extended to 10, but this will lengthen the induction.

Choose one word for the statement, for example, tiredness, or tension, or pain, or another word. Use it consistently, so that the person doesn't have to listen for a new word.

Preparation

It is helpful to give information at the start so that the person understands what will happen. The instruction may be worded as follows:

> I will count down from 5 to 1, and with each number you will feel more relaxed. At the end of the session I will reverse the counting, to help you return to a wakeful state.
>
> As soon as you feel comfortable you can close your eyes if you want to. This helps block out distracting light, and it helps focus your attention on your breathing, and this helps you to relax [this information gives a factual reason for closing eyes, and can help vulnerable people feel that they are safe and secure. If the person does not want to close their eyes, suggest they gaze at the floor].

The script

Begin the count-down (the ellipses indicate 2–3 seconds of silence between each phrase):

> 5 – becoming aware of your breathing...just notice the breath flowing easily in and out of your body...[pause]
>
> 4 – beginning to slow down your breathing now...taking slightly bigger and deeper breaths...feeling your body begin to relax...[pause]
>
> 3 – as you take deeper breaths, begin to notice how your chest and stomach fill out with the breath...and as you breathe out how the chest and shoulders fall...[longer pause]
>
> 2 – as you breathe out again be aware of releasing any tension/tiredness/pain [choose one of these] in your body and allow the tension/tiredness/pain [choose one] to flow out of the body...[longer pause]

> 1 – feeling more deeply relaxed...letting go of any tension/tiredness/pain [choose one]...allowing the breath to flow through the body easily, bringing a sense of comfort and relaxation to your whole body...[at this point start to play the music]. And now allow the music to be with you.

At the end of the music, begin the reverse cycle:

> The music has come to an end...stay with the relaxed feeling a little longer...
>
> 1 – still feeling relaxed...[pause]
>
> 2 – beginning to be aware of the sounds in the room...
>
> 3 – beginning to feel more alert now...[your voice becomes louder]
>
> 4 – feeling more alert and aware of what is around you...[voice at normal pace]
>
> 5 – feeling fully aware – opening your eyes and stretching your arms and legs.

AUTOGENIC INDUCTION

The ellipses indicate about 2–3 seconds of silence between the phrases.

Preparation

> Allowing your eyes to close gently...becoming aware of your breathing... and the cycle of taking in the breath and releasing it...notice the movement in your chest and stomach as you take in the breath, and as you release all the air from your chest... Notice how your body is feeling...you might feel your body is beginning to feel lighter, or it might be heavier...both of these feelings are fine... Gradually allow yourself to take deeper breaths... gently taking in the breath...gently releasing the breath... Allowing the breath to fall into its own natural pattern...

The script

> As you continue to breathe deeply, become aware of the muscles in your right foot...relax those muscles, so that your right foot feels gently relaxed... Become aware of the muscles of your right leg...relax those muscles, so that your right leg feels gently relaxed... Become aware of the muscles of your left foot...relax those muscles, so that your foot is relaxed... Become aware of the muscles of your left leg...relax those muscles, so that your left leg is relaxed... Become aware of the muscles through your hips and pelvis and through to the lower back...relax those muscles, so that this part of your body is relaxed... Become aware of the muscles of your stomach... relax those muscles, so that your stomach is relaxed... Become aware of the muscles in your diaphragm and chest...relax those muscles, so that your chest is relaxed... Become aware of the muscles of your shoulders, across the shoulders and the back of the shoulders...relax those muscles, so that your shoulders are relaxed... Become aware of the muscles of your arms through to your hands, and fingers and thumbs...relaxing those muscles, so that your arms and hands are relaxed. Become aware again of the muscles of your shoulders and, moving up now into the neck and throat...relax those muscles, so that your neck is relaxed... Become aware of the muscles of the face...the jaw, across the nose, the muscles of your eyes and behind your eyes, the forehead, to the top of your head...relax those muscles, so that your face is relaxed... And now feel the body fully and deeply relaxed... and now allow the music to be with you in this relaxed place...

This induction can be given in reverse order, from the head down to the feet.

End of the music:

A suggested script to return the client to a non-altered state of consciousness is:

> The music has finished...become aware of the sounds around you...the sounds inside the room, and the sounds outside of the room... Become aware of the room we are in...[and the people with you in the room for group sessions]... Begin to move your body, stretch out your arms...and legs... Take a deep breath...[the therapist might model an audible release

> of breath]... And have a yawn [the therapist might model this audibly]... And when you are ready, open your eyes...

AUTOGENIC RELAXATION WITH COLOUR

Colour can also be used in an autogenic induction. The client chooses a colour that they would like to breathe through the body. The therapist suggests the client be aware of what the colour might bring to the body (peace, comfort, warmth etc., but it might also be energy, or a feeling of aliveness). The therapist asks the client to tell them what the colour is and uses the client's words during the induction. The therapist says, 'Take in as much of the colour as you need' so the client is not overwhelmed by the colour. The therapist can also repeat the key word for what the colour brings to the body.

The script might be:

> Allowing your eyes to close...becoming aware of your breathing...and the cycle of taking in the breath and releasing it... Notice the movement in your chest and stomach as you take in the breath, and as you release the breath from your chest... Notice how your body is feeling...you might feel your body is beginning to become lighter, or it might be heavier...both of these feelings are fine...gradually allow yourself to take deeper breaths... gently taking in the breath...gently releasing the breath... Allowing the breath to fall into its own natural pattern...
>
> As you continue to breathe deeply, bring to your mind the colour that you would like to take into your body... Take a moment to think of this colour...it may be a colour that resonates with how you feel right now...or it could be a colour that you would like to bring into your body right now... take a few moments to think of the colour...notice the shade of the colour, notice its texture...and what it brings to you. When you have the colour in your mind, can you tell me what it is? We will be taking this colour through the different parts of the body...and you can allow the colour to change if it needs to.
>
> And now, taking that colour down to both feet... Allow the colour to be drawn in through the soles of both feet, so that the colour fills both feet

> to the ankles... Now allow the colour to move gently through both legs... through the lower legs, the knees...upper part of the legs...to the hips... allowing the colour to bring the body what it needs... Now allow the colour to move through the hips and through to the lower back...allow the colour to be in this part of your body, taking as much as it needs... Now allow the colour to move through to the stomach...only taking in as much as it needs [this is especially important for the internal organs]... Allow the colour to move to the chest...taking in as much colour as it needs... Take the colour into the back...allowing the colour to move gently through the back, bringing whatever the back needs... Allow the colour to move through the shoulders...and down the arms...through the wrists to the hands...and the fingers...and thumbs...allowing the colour to bring what the body needs... And now, taking the colour upwards from the shoulders...letting the colour move gently through the neck and the throat...into the jaw...across the cheeks...into the eyes...behind the eyes...and up into the forehead...to the very top of your head... And now, feeling the colour through the whole body...if there is an area that needs more colour, taking the colour there now... And now, allow the music to be with you.

Return the client to a non-altered state of consciousness:

> The music has finished...become aware of the sounds around you...the sounds inside the room, and the sounds outside of the room... Become aware of the room we are in...[and the people with you in the room for group sessions]... Begin to move your body, stretch out your arms...and legs... Take a deep breath...[the therapist might model an audible release of breath]... And have a yawn [the therapist might model this audibly]... And when you are ready, open your eyes...

MINDFULNESS INDUCTION

Preparation

> Allow yourself to be as comfortable as you can, loosening any clothing... If there are any sounds that you are aware of outside this room, allow them to fade away, knowing that someone else is attending to them...and

if there are any sounds that you are aware of in this room, allow them to fade away, knowing that someone else is attending to them. Feel the support of the mat, chair or cushion...

The script

Become aware of your breathing... Notice the movement of air in and out through your nose and notice the movement of your diaphragm... You may like to place a hand on your chest to feel this movement. Notice the breath coming into your chest.

You don't have to do anything at all, just be present to the awareness of your chest and the breath coming into your chest...aware of the feel of your chest, aware of whatever sensations are there to be felt...aware of your breath coming into your chest.

On the out breath, let go your awareness of your chest, and move your awareness to your shoulders. Be present to your awareness of your shoulders, aware of the feel of your shoulders, whatever sensations are there to be felt. When ready, breathe into your shoulders.

On the out breath, let go your awareness of your shoulders, and move your awareness to your arms, the upper arms, the elbow, lower arms, wrists, hands and fingers. Be present to your awareness of your arms, aware of the feel of your arms, whatever sensations are there to be felt. When ready, breathe into your arms.

On the out breath, let go your awareness of your arms, and move your awareness to your neck. Just be present to your awareness of your neck, aware of the feel of your neck, whatever sensations are there to be felt. When ready, breathe into your neck.

On the out breath, let go your awareness of your neck, and move your awareness to your head. Just be present to your awareness of your head, aware of the feel of your jaw, cheeks, eyes and forehead, whatever sensations are there to be felt. When ready, breathe into your head.

Reconnect now to the breath in the diaphragm and then use the same script for the lower half of the body: abdomen, hips and buttocks, upper legs, lower legs and feet.

Allow the music now to come into your awareness.

USING 'LIGHT' WITHIN RELAXATION INDUCTIONS

There are two alternative inductions here, which are also autogenic scripts. In the first, the focal point is 'light' that travels through the body or over the body. The various parts of the body may still be mentioned, as this helps the client to calm all areas of the body. In the second, the radiating light induction, the 'light' radiates from a sense of the centre of the person's self. It can be the 'soul' or the 'core of the self'.

Light induction

PREPARATION

Get yourself into a comfortable position...loosen anything that restricts your breathing [belts, tight collars, etc.]... Feel the support of the mat [or floor] for your body...feel the support for the head, shoulders, the spine and back...the arm and hands...the hips, legs and feet. Allow yourself to sink into the mat [or floor], beginning to let go of any tension held in the body... Allow the eyes to close gently...

Become aware of your breathing...it may be quite fast and irregular... just notice the pattern of your breathing, following the breath into your body and its release from your body...gradually allow yourself to take deeper breaths...gently taking in the breath...gently releasing the breath... allowing the breath to fall into its own natural pattern...

THE LIGHT SCRIPT

And now bring to your mind a sense of a ball of light...take a moment to allow the image to form in your mind...notice if the ball of light has a colour...allow the ball of light to hover over the top of your head...and as you breathe in next, allow the ball of light to move slowly over your head...allowing the light to fill this part of your body...taking in as much as you need... Allow the ball of light to move slowly and gently through your face and neck...taking in as much of the light as you need...allow the ball of light to move across the shoulders...down the arms...through to the hands...and fingers...to the very tips of the fingers...allow the light to move gently through the chest...taking in as much of the light as is

> comfortable...sensing the light through the chest, and through to the spine...through the lungs...and stomach...taking as much as you need... through to the pelvis and the lower back...taking as much as you need. Allow the light to move through the legs...the upper parts of the legs... the knees, the lower parts of the legs, to the feet and toes. Feel the glow of the light through your body...and now become aware of the music, and what the music brings to your body...

Start the music.

The light induction can also be given as radiating through the body. It brings awareness to the very centre of the person's being. Most often this is the solar plexus point in the centre of the breastbone. However, it is important not to assume that this is the central point – it may be the centre of the face for one person, or the stomach for another. Therefore, the induction leaves the actual site of the 'core of being' open. This induction is not suitable for people who may feel overwhelmed by breathing light into the body, such as those who are physically ill or vulnerable people. It is a powerful induction to use in that it focuses on the person's core being, and can be very empowering for clients when used at the right time. The induction fills the body with light, and for some clients the sensation might cause them to feel literally enlarged or inflated. The phrases 'take in as much as you need', or 'take in as much as is comfortable' are important to guard against feeling overly inflated. The induction is best suited to clients who are experienced in using relaxation inductions, and who can monitor the flow of suggestions.

Radiating light induction

This is a more advanced relaxation induction using light radiating through the body, and is best used with clients who will know how to imagine the radiating light.

PREPARATION

> Get yourself into a comfortable position...loosen anything that restricts your breathing [belts, tight collars, etc.]... Feel the support of the mat [or

> floor] for your body...feel the support for the head, shoulders, the spine and back...the arm and hands...the hips, legs and feet. Allow yourself to sink into the mat [or floor], beginning to let go of any tension held in the body... Allow the eyes to close gently... Become aware of your breathing...it may be quite fast and irregular...just notice the pattern of your breathing, following the breath into your body and its release from your body...gradually allow yourself to take deeper breaths...gently taking in the breath...gently releasing the breath...allowing the breath to fall into its own natural pattern...

THE RADIATING LIGHT SCRIPT

> And now, beginning to be aware of the centre part of your being...take a few moments to feel where the centre of your being might be...allow yourself to feel that core part of yourself, the very centre of who you are... take a few moments to sense where this centre is in your body...and when you have found that core place, breathe into that core place, allowing it to become alive...and now imagine a ray of light entering this core part of yourself...allow the light to radiate from the core place, gently filling the area around the core of your being...filling it with as much light as you need...gradually allow the light to radiate from this centre...gradually moving through the areas of the body...moving slowly and gradually through the cells...filling the body with the light of your core being...allow the light to radiate through to the head...the arms, hands and fingers... through to the spine...to the legs and feet...feeling the body filled with light...and now become aware of the music, and bring the music into this core of your being...

Start the music.

PROGRESSIVE MUSCLE RELAXATION (PMR) (BASED ON JACOBSON 1938)

The main feature of this induction is that it focuses on physically tensing and releasing the muscle groups throughout the body. This induction may be more successful with clients who prefer instructions. It is also very useful for clients who have a high degree of energy, for whom lying on the floor trying to imagine their muscles relaxing might be difficult. PMR is also useful for people who tend to need more clear and concrete instructions and guidance.

Conversely, people who prefer more creativity in their thinking might find the instructions too direct, and may 'resist' the instructions. As you become more practised with relaxation inductions an intuitive sense of which induction works best for which setting will be developed. The essential skill in the PMR sequence is to use the same timing for the instruction 'tighten'. If you systematically say 'tighten' twice (or three times) for each part of the body, the client can 'time' the tightening of the muscles. If you vary the number of times you say 'tighten', the client will be unsure how long each one lasts.

Voice tone

When you repeat the word 'tighten', your voice might be slightly louder to parallel the increase in the tension, but don't overdo it.

Preparation

> Get into a comfortable position...loosen anything that restricts your breathing [belts, tight collars, etc.]... Feel the support of the mat [or floor] for your body...feel the support for the head and shoulders...for the spine and back...the arms and hands...the hips, legs and feet. Allow yourself to sink into the mat [or floor], beginning to let go of any tension held in the body. Allow the eyes to close gently...become aware of your breathing... gradually allow yourself to take deeper breaths...gently taking in the breath...gently releasing the breath...allowing the breath to fall into its own natural pattern...

Script

> And now focus on the muscles in your right foot...tense the muscles of the foot, by drawing the foot back towards the body... Tense the muscles

tighter...tighter...and relax. Tense the muscles of your right leg, right up to the hip...tense the muscles tighter...tighter...and relax. Tense the muscles of your left foot...tense the muscles tighter...tighter...and relax. Tense the muscles of your left leg...tense the muscles tighter...tighter...and relax. Draw in the muscles through your pelvis, through to the lower back...draw in the muscles, tighter...tighter...and relax. Draw in the muscles of the stomach... tense the muscles tighter...tighter...and relax. Draw your shoulders forward to tense the muscles of the chest...tense the muscles tighter...tighter...and relax. Draw your shoulders back to tense the muscles of your back...tense the muscles tighter...tighter...and relax. Tense the muscles of your hands, by clenching the hands...tense the muscles tighter...tighter...and relax. Tense the muscles of the arms up to the shoulders by stretching them out... tense the muscles tighter...tighter...and relax. Tense the muscles of your shoulders by pulling them up towards the ears...tense the muscles tighter... tighter...and relax. Tense the muscles of the neck by raising the head off the pillow and stretching towards the chest...tense the muscles tighter... tighter...and relax. Tense the muscles of the jaw by clenching your teeth... tense the muscles tighter...tighter...and relax. Tense the muscles of your eyes, by scrunching up the eyes...tense the muscles tighter...tighter...and relax. Tense the muscles of the forehead by making a frown...tense the muscles tighter...tighter...and relax. And now be aware of how your body feels... Feel the body fully relaxed, allowing any last tension to be released from the body... And now listen to the music as it begins to play.

Start the music.

This induction can be given in reverse order, from the head down to the feet.

Bringing the client back to an 'alert' state

The music has finished... Become aware of the sounds around you...the sounds inside the room, and the sounds outside of the room... Become aware of the room we are in...and the people with you in the room... Begin to move your body, stretch out your arms...and legs... Take a deep breath [the therapist might model an audible release of breath]... And when you are ready, open your eyes...

Appendix B

Music Choices for Relaxation

CLASSICAL MUSIC

CD collections

From Winter's Stillness, ABC Classics (Australia)

Meditations for a Quiet Night

Meditations for a Quiet Dawn

Secret Garden: *Songs from a Secret Garden*

Tranquility Volumes 1 and 2, ABC Classics (Australia)

Short selections (note: duration timings will differ between different recordings)

Albinoni: *Concerto for oboe in D minor*, adagio, 5:23

Bach: *Brandenburg Concerto no. 6*, adagio ma non tanto, 5:29

Bach: *Christmas Oratorio*, 'Shepherd's song', 5:55

Bach: *Suite no. 3*, Air, 5:15

Beethoven: *Piano Concerto no. 5*, adagio, 7:45

Bizet: *Carmen*, intermezzo, 2:32

Borodin: *Symphony no. 1*, andante, 6:12

Butterworth: *The Banks of Green Willow*, 6:07

Debussy: *Dances Sacred and Profane*, 8:00

Delius: *1st Aquarelle*, 2:28

Dvořák: *Czech Suite*, 'Romanze', 4:32

Elgar: *Cello concerto*, adagio, 4:55

Elgar: 'Sospiri', 4:30

Fauré: *Requiem*, 'In *Paradissum*', 3:17

Fauré: *Pavane*, 7:47

Gluck: *Orfeo and Euridice*, 'Dance of the blessed spirits', 2:44

Grieg: *Cradle Song*, 4:07

Grieg: *Holberg Suite*, 'Air', 5:44

Grieg: *Peer Gynt Suite*, 'Morning', 4:00

Grieg: *Peer Gynt Suite*, 'Solveig's song', 5:00

Holst: *The Planets Suite*, 'Neptune', 7:01

Holst: *The Planets Suite*, 'Venus', 8:07

Korngold: *Much Ado about Nothing*, 'Garden scene', 4:38

Mascagni: *Cavelleria Rusticana*, intermezzo, 2:59

Massenet: *Thais*, 'Meditation', 5:47

Mozart: *Eine Kleine Nachtmusik*, 'Romance', 6:03

Pachelbel: *Canon in D*, 7:07

Puccini: *Madame Butterfly*, 'Humming chorus', 2:46

Rachmaninov: *Songs op. 34*, 'Vocalize', 6:51

Ravel: *Pavane*, 7:44

Ravel: *Piano concerto in G*, adagio, 8:59

Respighi: *The Birds Suite*, 'The dove', 4:30

Respighi: *The Birds Suite*, 'The nightingale', 4:30

Respighi: *The Fountains of Rome*, 'Villa Guilia at dawn', 4:28

Respighi: *The Fountains of Rome*, 'Villa Medici at sunset', 5:45

Saint-Saëns: *The Carnival of the Animals*, 'Aquarium', 2:34

Saint-Saëns: *The Carnival of the Animals*, 'The swan', 3:07

Shostakovich: *Piano Concerto no. 2*, andante, 7.36

Sibelius: *Scaramouche*, 4:06

Sor: *Etude op. 35 no. 2 for guitar*, 2:20

Stamitz: *Cello Concerto no. 2 in A*, 'Romance', 6:51

Tchaikovsky: *Romance in F minor*, 5:46

Warlock: *Capriol Suite*, 'Pieds en l'air', 2:21

Westlake: *Antarctica Suite*, 'Wooden ships', 4:16

Longer selections (approximately 8–10+ minutes)

Bach: *Concerto for Two Violins*, largo, 8:56

Beethoven: *Romance no. 2 in F major*, 9:47

Chopin: *Piano Concerto no. 1 in E minor*, 'Romance', larghetto, 9:19

Corigliano: *Voyage*, 8:41

Debussy: *Prelude to the Afternoon of a Faun*, 10:30

Dvořák: *Romance in F minor*, 12:46

Haydn: *Cello Concerto in C*, adagio, 9:45

Liadov: *The Enchanted Lake*, 7:58

Mozart: *Concerto for Flute and Harp*, andantino, 9:40

Mozart: *Piano Concerto no. 20 in D minor*, 'Romance', 9:00

Ravel: *Introduction and Allegro for Harp and Orchestra*, 10:17

Ravel: *Mother Goose Suite, Sleeping Beauty, Pavane and Fairy Garden*, 6:00

Ravel: *Piano concerto in G*, adagio, 8:59

Minimalist

Arvo Pärt: *Spiegel im Spiegel*, 10:30

Eric Satie: *Gymnopaedie*, no. 1 (3:36) and no. 3 (4:54)

Ludovico Einaudi: *I Giorni* [*The Days*], 5:59 (can fade out at 2:16)

Max Richter: *In the Garden*, 5:16

Max Richter: *On the Nature of Daylight* (30 minutes in total, but can be faded out)

Philip Glass: *Metamorphosis II*, 7:30

Philip Glass: *Tissue 7*, 3:14

CONTEMPORARY VOCAL

John Williams: 'Hymn to the Fallen' (Voces8)

Morten Lauridsen: *O Magnum Mysterium*

Ola Gjeilo: *Serenity*

Ola Gjeilo: *The Spheres*

Trad. 'Es ist ein Ros entsprungen' ['Lo, how a rose e'er blooming'] (Voces8)

FILM MUSIC

Benny Andersson: *Song from the Second Floor*, 3:47

Ennio Morricone: *The Mission* ('Gabriel's oboe', 2:12; 'Brothers', 1:30)

John Barry: Theme from *Out of Africa*, 3:10

Luis Bacalov: Theme from *Il Postino [The Postman]*, 2:43

Mozart: *Piano Concerto no. 21*, from *Elvira Madigan*, andante, 7:15

Stanley Myers: 'Cavatina', from *The Deer Hunter*, 4:12

William Walton: 'Touch her soft lips and part', from *Henry V*, 1:51

NEW AGE

Daniel Kobialka: *Going Home*

Daniel Kobialka: *Timeless Motion*

Enya: *Shepherd Moons* (tracks 3, 6, 9 and 10)

Enya: *Watermark* (tracks 1, 3, 6 and 8)

Liquid Mind: *Serenity*

Michael Hoppé: *Renouncement*

Michael Hoppé: *The Unforgetting Heart*

Secret Garden: 'Dreamcatcher', *Songs from a Secret Garden*

Secret Garden: 'Papillon', *Songs from a Secret Garden*

Secret Garden: 'White stones', *Home*

Steven Halpern: *Natural Light*

Steven Halpern: *Soft Focus*

Appendix C

Imagery Scripts for Children

These additional scripts are for hospitalized children aged approximately eight and above. The scripts are longer than the ones in Chapter 7 and therefore the music choice can be longer.

The ellipses indicate a pause in reading the script to allow the words to be processed. The pause might be 3–5 seconds depending on how the child is responding. In each example the music continues on after the script is finished, to the end of recorded piece of music, or continue improvising until you feel the child is more relaxed.

WHITE CLOUD INDUCTION

> [Music commences] Imagine that you are resting on a huge fluffy white cloud... The cloud is like a big pillow and it holds you really snugly and warmly... Imagine that the cloud is moving slowly in the sky...and you can see other clouds passing you by... On the other clouds there are some of your friends... Who can you see?... Maybe the clouds have different colours... What colours can you see?... And now your cloud is coming down from the sky very slowly...and it is coming down to the earth... slowly...slowly...slowly...and now it is resting on the ground...and you can hop off if you want to. [Music continues to the end]

SNOW LAND INDUCTION

This induction is effective for a child who has a fever and is feeling hot.

> [Music commences] Imagine that you are in a place called Snow Land. In Snow Land everything is made of snow... The trees are made of snow... The houses are made of snow... The animals are made of snow... Even the people are made of snow... You can feel the snow in your hands...and it's cool to touch... After a while you come to a place where there are many snow people smiling and saying hello to you... They know who you are... They are making a snowman out of the snow and they ask you to give them something to put on it... You give them a special present and they are very happy... So the snow people give you a present too... It's wrapped up, and it's something you've wanted for a long time... Carefully unwrap the present from the snow people and see what it is they have given you. [Music continues to the end]

A PINE FOREST INDUCTION

> [Music commences] Imagine you are entering a pine forest...beautiful tall, green pine trees are reaching up towards the sun...it is a warm sunny day. Feel the peacefulness of the tall trees...and imagine yourself walking towards them...look at the strong trunks of the trees...can you touch them?... Imagine you can hear the breeze as it whistles through the trees... Imagine yourself walking through the trees to a clear space...feel the sun on your body now...warm and gentle...and now you see an animal that has come into the clearing...it is a very friendly animal and it comes up close to you...you can stroke the animal if you like...feel how good your body feels now. [Music continues to the end]

SUNRISE OVER THE OCEAN INDUCTION

> [Music commences] Imagine you are looking out over the ocean...it is early in the morning...you see the sun coming up over the water...slowly

the yellow sun appears, getting larger and larger...you can feel the warmth of the sun's rays beginning to float over your body...you feel the gentle sun on your head...and across your shoulders...you feel the warmth of the sun down your arms and hands...you feel the sun down your back and your tummy...you feel the warmth of the sun down your legs and across your feet, and you feel the warmth of the sand under your feet. Now the sun is high up in the sky...and your body feels very warm. [Music continues to the end]

CLIMBING A MOUNTAIN INDUCTION

[Music commences] Imagine that you are standing at the foot of a mountain...look up at the mountain...and see its colour and its shape...you notice there is a small path that begins at the foot of the mountain...you begin to walk along the path...there are flowers by the side of the path, and small trees...and it is very green. The path begins to take you up the mountain... you can walk easily and you don't feel out of breath...up you go, higher and higher...as you get to the top of the mountain you can see a wonderful view...have a look around you and at the scenery from the top of the mountain...you can see forever...and you feel really happy...and now it is time to come down the mountain again...gently you begin to go back down the path...you feel very relaxed...you get back to the foot of the mountain and there is someone special there to meet you...they are very glad to see you. [Music continues to the end]

See Appendix B for a list of music choices.

Subject Index

Author Index